Grammar School Boy

Grammar School Boy

A Lincolnshire Education

Ronald J. Hill

First published in 2014
by
Clifden Gate Publications
2 Gatehouse Close
Clifden, Co. Galway
Ireland
EMAIL: clifdengate@eircom.net

Distributed by
York Publishing Services
64 Hallfield Road
Layerthorpe
York YO31 7ZQ
www.yps-publishing.co.uk

Typeset in Cambria 10.5 on 14 point by Lorton House

A CIP record for this book
is available from the British Library

ISBN 978-0-9929911-0-4

2 4 6 8 10 9 7 5 3 1

Contents

Acknowledgements

In offering this memoir I have many debts that I am all too happy to acknowledge.

The first is to my late parents, who suffered me and each other, did their very best in difficult, at times trying, circumstances, and supported my endeavours as far as they were able, even though the education that they encouraged led me in directions that they could not follow and changed me in ways that they found baffling. May they rest in peace. I should add that much of the detail in this account would have been absent but for the rich hoard of letters, photos and school exercise books that my mother retained for years and left behind.

The second is to my teachers in the three schools that I attended until shortly after my eighteenth birthday, when I entered Leeds University at the start of a life in higher education that has been at times challenging, but exceptionally rewarding. It has allowed me to visit and live in interesting places, meet genuinely inspiring people, and, I hope, make a difference to the lives of students and others. My schools no longer exist, at least as I knew them, but they are indelibly fixed in my mind, and I look back with fondness to the dedicated educators who set me on my path.

An equally influential element in my education derived from the interests and hobbies that I pursued and developed: playing in a skiffle group, engaging with the Scouts, train-spotting, I-Spy, correspondence with penfriends. Countless cousins, classmates, youth leaders and friends opened my eyes and mind during my formative years. Many may have forgotten me, yet I am grateful, years after their influence waned, for their contribution to my intellectual development.

In particular, I thank former students, friends and colleagues who have encouraged me in this task. I thank especially three former schoolmates: Brian Moss, Rhieta Prowle, *née* Lewis, and Joy Rushby, *née* Appleyard;

Rhieta's husband Allen, poet and translator; and former colleagues at Essex University, David Stephen and the late Professor Peter Frank, whom I knew before that as a student colleague at Leeds. My brother John, who features in these pages, also helped jog my memory; to him and his wife Margaret I am extremely grateful. All these kind friends generously undertook to read the whole book and offered valuable criticism and advice (not all of which I accepted!). I absolve them of responsibility for any lapses of my memory or judgement that may have impaired this account.

Finally, my biggest thanks go to my wife, Ethna Frayne, who has not only tolerated my obsession with getting this story written and published, but has even encouraged me in the process. She read multiple drafts, offered her considered opinion, and was still happy that I pressed on. I dedicate the book to her, with love.

R.J.H.

Dublin, July 2014

Prologue

I was a beneficiary of the 1944 Education Act, introduced in the year after I was born by R. A. ('RAB') Butler. My purpose in writing this memoir is to record the effect on the lucky minority of children in the 1940s and '50s who were admitted to state Grammar Schools, and the transformative effect of education in its broadest sense.

My story is, on the face of it, not unusual. It is set in North Lincolnshire – or, more precisely near the south bank of the Humber in the former division of Lindsey – yet hundreds of thousands of British children had similar experiences. They took their 11-plus selection examination at the end of primary school and were thereafter segregated for the rest of their schooling. Those deemed to possess academic potential went to the Grammar School; those with supposed technical skills went to a Technical School; and the rest went to Secondary Modern.

It is a well-known story, and it became clear early on that selection for the Grammar School was seen as an individual success. Secondary Modern was perceived as failure, and it affected those who went there throughout their lives. The 'Technical Schools' were something of an enigma. My younger brother John attended one, by choice, and the experience did not serve him well. True, there was some 'technical' content in the curriculum: rather more training in woodwork than I received, plus metalwork (not available to me), and technical drawing (which I studied for one year). But his undeniable talents went undeveloped – possibly unrecognised – and his formal qualifications after five years were at best disappointing. They hardly trained him for the world of work, and certainly did not equip him for a life of social advancement to positions of responsibility. He and his generation could find work, by and large, and perhaps most did not resent their position; but their bosses mostly went to grammar schools. In that system, there were few opportunities for mistakes to be rectified; some pupils were 'demoted' from Grammar to Secondary Modern; movement in the opposite direction was very uncommon. One or two individuals did transfer to my Grammar School after a couple of years in a Secondary Modern; one in particular, having missed the first two or three years of French, used Linguaphone to teach himself the basics, overtook the rest of us, and went on to shine in that subject. But such instances were rare.

The three-tiered system of secondary education was ultimately deemed a failure. Socially divisive and ineffectual in motivating the bulk of British youth to identify their potential and strive to achieve it, Grammar, Technical and Secondary Modern schools gave way from the mid-1960s to 'comprehensive' schooling, without 'streaming' at the age of 11 (although this system itself became subject to other forms of selection, including the notorious postcode definition of catchment areas, from the 1990s).

The 11-plus allowed me to escape from the life of drudgery, hard work and limited expectations that my parents suffered. Without it, I suspect, I might never have had the courage – and my family would never have had the supporting financial resources – to aspire to a career in academia that has proved immensely rewarding, and has allowed me to travel the world, meet interesting people, write and publish books and articles in several countries and languages, and pursue matters that engaged my interest rather than being told what to do. I am one of the lucky minority of the minority. I assume I possess a modicum of native talent: but without the possibilities afforded by RAB's Education Act, I doubt whether I should have moved far from North Lincolnshire.

My roots still lie there – at least to the extent that I have not put down deep roots elsewhere, even though my career has taken me away. At the age of eighteen I left to study Russian at Leeds University, and from October that year, 1961, my contacts with 'home' diminished, as I moved away in pursuit of work and a career. Upon graduation, I moved to Colchester, Essex, to the new university that was attempting to establish its scholarly reputation by engaging research assistants, a position to which I was appointed to work on a project on Soviet politics. To ease the transition into the social sciences, I simultaneously took a master's programme in Political Behaviour, followed by a year as an exchange student in Kishinev, capital of the Soviet republic of Moldavia, where I lived among Soviet citizens, improved my Russian, and gathered materials for my doctoral thesis.

By the time the degree of PhD was conferred, by Lord Butler of Saffron Walden, as RAB had become, I had already embarked on an academic career in Trinity College, Dublin, where I had been appointed a Junior Lecturer in 1969. I progressed up the career ladder and retired as a professor in 2007, by which time I had also been elected one of the seven Senior Fellows.

All of this kept me away from North Lincolnshire, apart from visits to my parents and brother in Scunthorpe and sporadic visits to other family members who remained nearby. I tried to follow what was going on the region, but over half a century I grew away.

Yet I remember vividly many of the incidents and influences that formed my mind and determined my outlook on life and the world, including not only the formal 'education' in the classroom but, equally important, the interests and activities that I pursued outside school. One of the main lessons of my experience, which I try to capture in this memoir, is that the search for 'relevance' in a school curriculum is itself pretty irrelevant. No one knows what skills will be of value one, two or three decades into a working career, or what knowledge or experience – whether gained in the classroom or through hobbies and social interactions – will contribute to successful work or pleasure later in life.

What my story also shows, however, is the distancing effect of education. Not only in the sense that higher education, in particular, often leads to a career away from where one has been nurtured as a child, but also in the sense that the social mobility that accompanies education may have an alienating effect. Friends and family become remote, and both sides lose.

Revisiting North Lincolnshire, after two-thirds of a lifetime that offered few opportunities to retain contacts, evokes curious memories, because so many of the details have disappeared. Not only have villages become towns and towns been transformed by demolition and rebuilding, but many of the people I knew have passed on, moved away, or indeed changed in ways that would render them unrecognisable if I met them unexpectedly. I too have changed, of course, so probably no one would know me if we met casually on Pelham Road, Immingham, and the stories of our lives would display occasional similarities and wide divergences.

The second half of the twentieth century, the period of human history in which I myself formed part of a link in the chain, was undoubtedly one of significant change. It is highly unlikely that any future generation of English boys and girls will experience that life again – the Britain of the 1950s has gone.

This memoir is not my life story. Neither is it a pathetic *cri de coeur* for a return to something that was lost but cannot be recaptured. Rather it is an account of the experience of one individual who at a particular time in the history of the country and the world was enabled by circumstances to change his life chances. The changes in my life wrought by education were interpreted as a success for me as an individual, as I evolved from railwayman's son to professor. Yet those changes effectively undermined the solidarity of the communities from which I sprang: family, village, class, county and in my case – having devoted my energies to educating the young of a neighbouring country – my motherland. As I myself became transformed, the milieu in which my journey began also changed, so my connections with my roots became ever more tenuous.

But I begin with my parents' generation, to illustrate the magnitude of the change in my fortunes.

1

Son of a Lost Generation

Dick and Elsie, my parents, were from North Lincolnshire, born immediately after the First World War. They regarded themselves as belonging to a lost generation. Both came from a large family by today's standards. My father was the eighth of a dozen children of a farm foreman who died when Dad was seventeen; my grandmother, a widow at fifty or so, took in washing to support her family, and my father left school at fourteen to do farm work. Richard (members of his family used his full name) joined the railway company in April 1937, the start of a career that embraced 44 years of railway service and culminated in a decade as a driver of diesel locomotives. A photo from those early years shows him wearing what later became his trademark railway cap and leaning proudly against a locomotive that he had just finished polishing. Given the assumptions of the previous half-century, he probably felt he was set to work his way up to become a member of the working-class aristocracy as a train driver.

My mother was the fifth and youngest child of Albert Wilkinson Wilson, a skilled cabinet maker and trained piano and organ tuner, who earned a modest living as a painter and decorator but had much wider mechanical skills. On the living room wall of his house in Cleethorpes there hung an electric clock, which he had made from whatever came to hand: the case crafted in mahogany and glass, the face fashioned from a metal dinner plate that he had flattened; the drive mechanism included a pendulum and a small bath of mercury that served as an electrode. Years earlier, he had made a radio for his teenage son, Arthur, who was blind: it could be switched on and off by simply sliding the 'works' like a drawer

JOHN WILLIAM HILL, c. 1935

FLORENCE MARY HILL, 1942

ALBERT AND ELEANOR MARY WILSON, c. 1903

THE WILSON FAMILY, 1927

HERBERT FLORENCE ('FLORRIE')

ELEANOR MARY EDNA ARTHUR ELSIE ALBERT WILKINSON

into and out of its casing. He had also experimented with various loud-speakers in the sitting room to hear classical music on the BBC to best advantage. His eldest son, my Uncle Herbert, inherited the Wilson mechanical gene: when, in his sixties, he had to have the lenses removed from both eyes, he astounded optometrists by grinding and polishing suitable lenses from Perspex. Albert became a widower when my mother was a small girl. As her elder sisters married and left, she undertook ever more responsibility for running the family home, including having to explain to the rent-collector that her father had a big job on, so would have to delay payment until the following week.

The depression of the 1930s hit such families very hard. Food was scarce; their clothing was cheap and old; shoes were sometimes lined with cardboard to cover holes in the sole. Even Christmas was a make-do affair: the 'bird' (usually a chicken) was bought at a reduced price just before the market closed on Christmas Eve, and my mother's family Christmas 'tree' was three interlocking wooden hoops covered in crepe paper, suspended from the ceiling and decorated with a few baubles – one reason my mother in later life always insisted on at least a symbolic small artificial tree.

Both parents, therefore, suffered the loss of one of their own parents in their childhood or youth, and were obliged to work. Despite their clear intelligence, for them education beyond the primary level was out of the question: they had to bring in money. When my mother left Reynolds Street school, Cleethorpes, in December 1933, after her fourteenth birth-day, her headmistress wrote a recommendation:

> Elsie Wilson is a very intelligent scholar & leaves this school in an 'A' Class. She has a quiet refined pleasant manner. She has proved herself efficient & trustworthy and can be thoroughly recommended. Attendances 109/114. Marks 83%.

Armed with this reference, she entered domestic service in the home of a Mrs Fell, and she later told the story of how on her first day at work she was asked to cook a cabbage. Never having been properly trained, she simply took off the outer leaves, put the cabbage into a saucepan and tried to boil it whole!

The recovery later in the 1930s brought modest relief. While Dick was setting off on a career away from the land, Elsie, in her off-duty hours, began to enjoy a pastime that later became a passion: singing. She had already won a school prize for story-telling, and as a teenager she joined the Cleethorpes Ladies' Choir, where her distinctive contralto voice and impressive ability to hold the descant line made her a stalwart as they performed locally and even travelled to the Blackpool musical festival on one occasion. Her family background was clearly one up in the hierarchy from that of my father. Albert Wilson was a craftsman, and he passed to Elsie bourgeois tastes in music and dress and an interest in ideas that the son of a hard-working farm labourer had not attained. Still, Dad must have had some ambition at the time, and he had managed to escape the harsh life of his own parents.

But the hopes stirred by the economic recovery were followed by the catastrophe of the Second World War. Elsie did farm work briefly as a 'Land Girl' in the Women's Land Army, while her elder sisters made camouflage nets in Grimsby. Dick was sent to France as a sapper with the British Expeditionary Force. His elder brother, Tom, was killed in Belgium on 16 May 1940, less than a week after the start of Hitler's Blitzkrieg which ended the 'Phoney War'; not long afterwards, my grieving grandmother received a second official telegram to say that her son Richard was missing in action, days after his twenty-first birthday.

Missing – but not killed. His company – the 272nd Field Company, Royal Engineers – was at Abbeville when the German forces attacked. The town fell swiftly, and British troops on one side of the town were captured and marched eastward as Prisoners of War. By coincidence, decades later, when Dad was volunteering as a lay assistant to the chaplain in Scunthorpe hospital, he met one of this group of former POWs, in hospital as a patient. On the 'leeward' side of the town, 272 Company was able to escape. Dad was rarely willing to talk about his war experiences, but towards the end of his life he quietly told me that they had been left more or less to their own devices, each man for himself, to get to the coast. They initially commandeered a train, which Dad managed to drive for a few miles while his companions jettisoned the cargo of cans of petrol, getting the company away from immediate danger. After the train crashed, they made their way on foot, some following the road, others the rail track. Walking by night, hiding by day, hearing German forces in their vicinity, scavenging for food, it was, he told me decades later, four days of 'sheer hell'.

They reached the port of Dieppe hoping for evacuation, and made themselves useful by working at the harbour, clearing medical supplies

RICHARD (DICK) HILL,
RAILWAYMAN, c. 1937

ELSIE WILSON, AGE 15

1890271 SAPPER R HILL

from a warehouse and avoiding the air raids. My father and a mate were offloading a heavy load of metal bottles when a siren signalled a raid. The mate panicked and dropped the crate, one end of which landed on my father's foot. He was treated in the garrison hospital, where he spent his twenty-first birthday – 29 May. He partially recovered from his injury (although he never regained full mobility), but caught food poisoning from the hospital food. After another devastating air raid, he was put on a train of horse boxes with comrades in a desperate effort to get to another port. Alas, the food poisoning took its toll on my father, who suffered a severe case of diarrhoea. With no toilet facilities available, he did as any soldier would do in the circumstances: he extended his posterior through the open sliding door and 'performed'. Unluckily for him, he did not know the line as he would later have to learn it as a train driver in civvy street. When the train entered a tunnel – well, suffice it to say that he was again badly injured, he bore the scars for life, and there is one corner of a railway tunnel in Northern France that will remain forever England. His separation from 272 Field Company while in hospital in Le Mans led to the report that he was missing.

He and his comrades eventually managed to get back to Blighty, after evacuation from St. Malo on 14 June, re-joined their unit, and following convalescence and a spell in Scotland Dad was put back to work on the railway, deemed a vital national occupation. He was assigned to the English Midlands, to the railway depot at Woodford Halse, in Northamptonshire, not far from the towns of Banbury and Daventry. Now a sprawling dormitory village that feeds to the M1 and M40 motorways, Woodford Halse was a significant point on the Great Central Line from London to the North, closed in the notorious 'Beeching cuts' that devastated the rail network in the 1960s. He was initially billeted in the house of a Mrs Pearcy, whom he visited for a number of years afterwards, occasionally taking me along.

My parents were married in a wartime wedding, after what appears to have been a fairly brief courtship that began at another wedding in 1941. Times were obviously hard for them and for everyone else in their social milieu. Dick, with a steady job on the railways, must have been seen as a suitable catch for any girl from a similar background, even (perhaps especially) one with a *paterfamilias* as strict and protective as my maternal grandfather. Elsie saw marriage as a way of escaping a life dominated by her severe Victorian father, and also looked for companionship. She cannot have understood that life with a shift worker, whose duties could begin at literally any minute of the night or day, was not going to be conducive to the kind of marriage that she craved.

She had apparently been in love with a man some years older than herself, Eddie, enlisted in the Ambulance Corps. My grandfather objected to this romance, probably because of the age difference. Yet even after her engagement to Dick, in letters to his lost love Eddie expressed his disappointment, explained why he had not pressed harder to win her hand, and gallantly expressed his best wishes for her happiness, and the hope that he might meet Dick one day.

Thanks to the discipline that her father imposed – redoubled, no doubt, when one of her sisters found herself pregnant before marriage – she had no experience of intimacy and was practically ignorant of sex (although there are persistent family rumours of abuse by Granddad). My father was not quite so ignorant, but was certainly inexperienced, and, no doubt under the influence of his very simple religious convictions, quite self-righteous about this. He had walked out of digs at one point when his landlady invited him to share her bed, and he had broken off an engagement to a previous love because he was not prepared to 'do what all her friends were doing' and evidently enjoying.

Shortly afterwards, on the rebound perhaps, he met Elsie, a very pretty young lady from a respectable family: early photographs show a very sweet child with a chirpy smile, and a teenager of enormously attractive good looks. Dick was quite handsome, courteous, modest, and he had a steady job with prospects. Granddad approved, and the couple were married in St. Aidan's Church, Cleethorpes, on 23 August 1942. Wartime austerity dictated a modest wedding. There was no official photographer, and the surviving snapshots of what appears to have been a happy couple are poorly composed and under-exposed; the silver horseshoes and lucky charms given to the bride were of cardboard; taxis to and from the church cost ten shillings each way, and the modest reception took place at the bride's home.

In fact, they were poorly matched from the start, with nothing much in common, even physically: my father stood at over six feet, whereas my mother barely made five feet tall: 'Little Else' was my brother's nickname for her in the early 1960s, following the success of the female rock singer Little Eva. My father was somewhat clumsy and lacking in finesse, incapable of tuning in a radio or hammering in a straight nail; my mother came from a family of talented, inventive, manually dexterous individuals with a fascination for things mechanical and a deep interest in music. She loved singing; my father could barely hold a tune (although he tried hard). She was keen to escape and to make use of her talents; he was unimpeachably conscientious, but had limited ambition. And I believe she was really in love with Eddie. Had my grandfather acquiesced in their love, she might never have met Dick, and I would not have been here. They might both have enjoyed happier lives than their sixty-odd years of stoically endured marriage afforded them.

They moved to Northamptonshire, in the vicinity of the Woodford Halse railway depot, and in quick succession they produced their family: myself, born less than a year after their wedding, and my brother John, born a year and a half later. At the end of the war they returned to civilian life in North Lincolnshire, with little but hope to sustain them. My father now had a job as a railway fireman, based at Barnetby, a significant railway junction; my mother, somewhat undernourished and sickly as a child, suffered a nervous breakdown sometime after my brother's birth, probably associated in part with recognition of the brutal truth that she had little love for the husband whose two children she had borne.

They muddled through, disappointed, frustrated, sometimes angry and ultimately resigned. Circumstances, they believed, had hampered their lives, and they hoped that their children might bring a kind of redemption. While my mother did eventually gain much enjoyment and satisfaction from singing and teaching, she lacked the wholehearted support of her husband, whose shift work offered an excuse for his own lack of interests or hobbies.

My own progress through school and life was a source of satisfaction combined with resentment when education led me in directions and into social milieus that left them both – and particularly my father – uncomfortable. They did not understand the effect of education on the individual. For Dad it was a means of getting a 'better' job and improving one's earning power, whereas it thoroughly transformed my outlook in ways that he found difficult to appreciate or accept. The estrangement that we as a family experienced was an unintended – or at least unforeseen – consequence of my social mobility, and it has left me with a residual sense of guilt towards a generation that always 'did its best' (a favourite phrase of my father) without a vision of where life was leading.

2

Born on the Fourth of July

I was born on the fourth of July 1943, when Britain and much of Europe were fighting for their existence, in a place with which none of my family had even the remotest connection. After his wartime experiences in France, followed by convalescence, a return to the railways, and marriage to Elsie, Dad's work kept him in the Midlands, shovelling coal on steam locomotives on the Great Central Line. The newly-weds lived in a succession of villages in Northamptonshire, renting one or two rooms here and there for ten or twelve shillings a week from sometimes unscrupulous landlords. When he wrote to the local council expressing his dismay at their treatment and requesting assistance, Dad's letter was read out at a council meeting and later reported in full in the local newspaper. The young couple were soon evicted and had to find accommodation in another village. It was an embarrassing and bitter lesson stemming from innocence and ignorance of the ways of the world.

Ten and a half months after their wedding I was born in Bragborough Hall, Braunston, a small manor house that had been taken over by the government for use as a maternity hospital, mainly by young women sent to the countryside for safety from the London area. Years afterwards, my mother remembered the 'horrible' registrar whose signature appears on my birth certificate: H. W. Porter. He conducted his business with each new mother in a loud voice in front of all the others in the makeshift ward, and thoroughly embarrassed several of them by asking, pointedly and patronisingly, 'And how long have you been married, my dear?'

My arrival in the world appears to have brought a little joy into my parents' lives. Elsie was the only young mother in the ward who definitely knew she wanted another baby – and presumably by that stage she knew what making babies entailed. After his first inspection visit, my father wrote to his 'own darling' a letter that reflected her 'excitement at the joy of having a boy'. He himself was delighted that I was born on American Independence Day, which he wrote was 'Best of All, *Our Day*'. He was, he wrote, 'too excited even if I wanted to sleep'. The next letter, a few days later, was addressed to 'Dearest Elsie & Ronald' – which reveals that very quickly the midwife's choice of name for their first child had been accepted. My mother wanted 'Ronnie', to which the midwife said: 'Why spoil a nice name like "Ronald"?' So Ronald it became – and I have disliked it ever since I became aware of it, although obviously not enough to change it by deed poll, or even to use my second name, James.

Perhaps the earliest family photograph, taken a few weeks after I was born, shows my father seated with me on his lap, my mother standing behind him. This was not a conventional family pose, and examination of my mother's dress reveals the reason: my incontinence, which not only created a dark stain, but caused the crepe fabric to wrinkle. Having her stand behind my father – who looks distinctly uncomfortable – was the photographer's way of largely hiding my efforts. I appear unconcerned.

My brother John was born in the village of Culworth, on Boxing Day 1944 – less than a year and a half after my own birth. Since Dad worked unpredictable shifts, and there were no local family members to give support, my mother's eldest sister Florrie came from Lincolnshire to assist her in the first few days. I was later told that within half an hour of John's birth I displayed early signs of precocity, or at least some facility with words. I could evidently form a complete sentence, because, as Auntie Florrie gave my infant brother a few drops of water from a teaspoon, I begged her, 'Give him a cup.'

However, the joy and excitement brought by the arrival of 'family' proved short-lived. Letters sent by my father to his fiancée and young wife – which she kept, probably unread for decades, till the end of her life – suggest that their relationship deteriorated very quickly. In later years, the emotional and sexual incompatibility all but destroyed the marriage. Indeed, it would not be inaccurate to say that it was less a marriage, more an arrangement, whereby Dad brought in the money, Mam ran the household, and they shared the same home. Acts of physical affection were extremely rare, and the relationship was characterised by

MY INCONTINENT SELF, OCTOBER 1943

scorn, disappointment and jealousy, my father constantly suffering sexual frustration and my mother enduring the dissatisfaction of not being given either the companionship she had hoped for or the loving appreciation that she needed in using her talents.

Perhaps this sense of early disenchantment in marriage, the loneliness inflicted by my father's shift work, combined with the difficult circumstances in which they lived, a long way from friends and family in Lincolnshire, contributed to my mother's nervous or mental breakdown within months of John's birth. I was sent to stay with my father's sister Ivy, who lived in Anstey, near Leicester, for several weeks. I remember little of that period, but it had quite an effect on me, not least in making me reluctant to accept my mother's affection. A few details I do recall from that and subsequent visits in infancy: in the bath – a luxury that had not existed in my life until then – I pretended I was swimming; the kettle whistling in the kitchen convinced me I had heard a train outside the house – which says something of how my consciousness had already been affected by living in a railwayman's family; walks to Bradgate Park, where Lady Jane Grey (queen for nine days in the sixteenth century) had lived, to climb the hill to the ruined tower known as Old John, and the return home through the woods and fields filling a bag with leaf mould for use as potting compost. And my first encounter with dentures had me pulling vigorously at my own front teeth in order to remove them. I always returned to the area with great fondness – without appreciating the sad reason for my initial visit.

Mercifully, I have no recollection of one of the potentially tragic events of my early life. It's not the kind of thing one would wish to remember, and my parents would have been forever struck with embarrassment if they had to explain how their first-born came to a sad end. Under the pressures of war, local services, never particularly abundant in rural England, were severely curtailed. In the absence of sewerage, primitive closets or privies – essentially very large buckets covered with a wooden seat – were the norm. In peacetime these were cleared weekly by tanker – in North Lincolnshire we called it 'the dilly cart' – and removed. During the war, such services had to be dispensed with, but the problem of disposal and treatment of the raw sewage remained. A common procedure was for the men in a small neighbourhood to dig a trench, empty the slops at night, let the liquid drain away and cover the remains in the morning.

On one morning, however, the covering had not been done when I was let out into the garden. I cannot have been two years old – a mere toddler – and I toddled right in the direction of the open trench and promptly fell in. I imagine it was not a pleasant experience for me – but since I lived to tell the tale (as recounted years later by my mother) I cannot have fallen face-down. My mother rescued me and carried me at arms' length back into the house and gave me a good scrubbing. In the austerity of the war years, there was no spare clothing. My little romper suit could not simply be thrown away into the trench and buried. My mother had the unenviable task of washing it, sterilising it and doing whatever else was needed to make the garment serviceable. My life continued apparently normally, but my mother never forgot – and I suspect she never let my father forget, either.

After the war, with the family back in North Lincolnshire, Dad would occasionally take me with him to visit his old landlady, Mrs Pearcy, no doubt to give my mother a break. From there I date some of my earliest memories.

'Old Ben' was a thatcher and general farmhand, who seemed very, very old. His hair was white under a battered hat, his cheeks and chin unshaven, and a luxuriant white moustache adorned his upper lip. He wore the typical clothing of a man in his position in those days: a collar-less shirt open at the neck, a waistcoat and trousers once part of a three-piece suit, and sturdy leather boots as comfortable as they were old.

I probably first met him in the summer of 1946, about the time of my third birthday, on one such visit, and again in the terrible winter of early 1947, when I distinctly remember 'helping' my father and others from the village to clear snow from the main road. The men had garden shovels; I was dressed in a heavy coat and a light brown knitted headpiece to cover my ears, and given a little coal shovel with which to help the adults. There is a photograph of this occasion, my father dressed, as usual, in his railway uniform cap, an item that he was rarely without, with another of the lodgers, taking a rest, and me by his side screwing up my eyes from the glare of the sun glinting off the snow. I sat on a layer of a couple of feet of snow from which Dad and his mate had already dug a vast amount, and I thought 'How like a settee.'

JANUARY 1947

A few months later, my father and I visited Mrs Pearcy again. The door was open, and sun streamed in. Hens and the occasional duck wandered in and out from the yard outside as we sat at the table. The enormous black cooking range set into a huge chimney place was used to prepare our meals. At the other side of the house, which I now recognise must have been the front, there was another door which I imagine opened on to the street. We always used the back entrance, but neighbours and other visitors would come to the front door. One such visitor was Monica, a little girl from a neighbouring house, a year or two older than I was, who evidently took a strong dislike to me because at our first meeting she sank her teeth into the back of my right hand, drawing blood. I have never trusted girls named Monica since then.

After we had settled down, and Dad had gone off to do whatever Dads and the other lodgers do when visiting their former landlady, I explored the garden area. 'Old Ben' was at the top of a ladder, repairing thatch on the roof. He and I obviously got on well. I felt comfortable enough to ask him to come down and help me unbutton my trousers to answer a call of nature. Down he came, willing to help because Dad was not around. I smiled at him and told him I didn't need to do any business. I'd caught him out! Back he climbed up the ladder, and my father and the other adults were entertained when Old Ben told them the story later.

Across the yard, to the right of the back door, was a high brick wall, with a lean-to greenhouse, somewhat dilapidated, in which nettles grew. A couple of days after tricking Old Ben, I wandered over there and had an early biology lesson: nettles sting and raise welts. But since I was alone, I was not taught the curative effect of dock leaves in counteracting a nettle sting. Rooting around inside the greenhouse I also spotted what I was later told was a rusty razor blade. I quickly learned another lesson: razor blades, rusty or not, can cut fingers if not carefully handled.

These visits to rural Northamptonshire continued for a few years, and my father regularly corresponded with Mrs Pearcy, whom we regarded as an informal aunt. She even came to visit us for lunch in the mid-1950s, in the company of a female companion whose Cockney accent had my brother and me in stitches right through the meal.

At the first stage of his military service, Dad had been billeted in Sheffield, in the home of a Mr and Mrs Sanders, of Blair Athol Road. After the war, Dad continued to correspond with the couple, and after Mr Sanders died we would visit his widow. We boys were encouraged to call her 'Auntie Sanders'. A kindly old lady, she was small, with a slight stoop, her silver hair tied back in a bun on her neck, wearing round glasses, and a warm smile, but, somewhat disconcertingly to small boys, her jaw trembled. Once or twice a year, the whole family would take the train from Barnetby or Habrough to Sheffield Victoria (which closed permanently in the early 1970s), and thence by Victorian bone-shaker tram beyond The Moor to Mrs Sanders's house.

Sheffield was the first city I ever encountered. There were still signs of bombing in the centre, and the air was thick with pollution from the coke ovens and furnaces of the iron and steel works that were helping the country to recover. The rows and rows of red-brick terraced houses that covered the hillsides outside the city centre were quite beyond my experience, and they impressed my village consciousness. The houses themselves seemed enormous, perhaps because of the proportions of the rooms and furniture, but with tiny back yards and gardens shared between each pair, a bird bath in this one, a flowering cherry tree in another, and inside – to my repeated delight – a cellar, where coal was kept. On every visit, I would ask to be allowed to descend the steep stone steps, just to look and wonder.

It was clear to us boys that this was a relatively well-to-do household compared with our own. The photographs of the couple showed Mr Sanders in a three-piece suit and a homburg, with a gold watch chain linking the pockets of his waistcoat; the furniture included antiques; and the item that most fascinated me was a Victorian picture in which a mountain scene was framed with shimmering butterflies' wings. It had probably been imported from India or somewhere equally exotic. My father believed that he had been promised it as a memento when Mrs Sanders died, and he occasionally expressed regret and disappointment that it did not come his way when she passed on in the 1960s.

Snatches of conversation among the adults conveyed the mood of those years of austerity and rationing. 'Auntie Sanders' loved cheese, and bemoaned the fact that her ration was a mere two ounces a week; and with what must have contained a hint of envy, a comment from my father that she would walk from one tram stop to the next in order to save a ha'penny – the implication being that such 'stingy' behaviour was the way the 'well-off' hung on to their wealth. After her husband's death her constant companion was her budgie, Billy. She chatted to him all through the day as she went about her chores, he chatted back in phrases that we could sometimes discern – 'Good boy, Billy' or 'Billy's tired' – and he was occasionally allowed out of his cage to fly around the dining room for our amusement.

The episode with the latrine trench and its aftermath evokes the primitive nature of rural life in the wartime and early post-war years. Electrical gadgets had been invented, but they were not in common use. Washing was a hard day's work for most housewives, usually tackled on a Monday, except in my household, where my mother preferred Tuesday. From my fifth year, when we moved into our first complete dwelling (literally two up, two down), my mother would be up early (Dad was as often as not at work on a night shift) to light a fire under a copper kettle built into a brick encasement in the small kitchen, and carry several bucketfuls of water from the hand pump that served as the water supply for four cottages. The sheets and cotton garments would be boiled – my mother boasted that after a few washes her sheets were whiter than when new – and the rest whisked around in a galvanised tub with the aid of 'dolly pegs': what looked like a four-legged low stool attached to a broom handle with a crosspiece handle at the top, that could be spun in both directions to turn the washing in the tub of hot water and soap powder – Oxydol, Rinso and Tide were the brands of that era. The washed garments and linen would be passed through a mangle, its rollers turned by hand, and then rinsed several times – the last time with a hint of blue in the water; shirts were also dipped from the waist up in a bowl of starchy water – before being finally wrung through the mangle and hung out on the line strung the length of the garden path.

It was all very demanding and human energy-consuming. The acquisition of manual washing machines – in which the agitation of the clothing was done by a paddle inside the cylinder, turned back and forth by a handle attached to the central spindle – barely reduced the effort required: it simply made it more convenient. The automatic washing machine and non-iron fabrics were far ahead in the future.

Shopping, too, was a time-consuming and onerous task. No driving to the supermarket on a Saturday morning to buy a whole week's provisions. The supermarket may already have been invented, across the Atlantic, but England in the forties and fifties was still in the 'Open All Hours' mode. Shop assistants were more than check-out till operators. Most food shops were specialist in those years: butchers, with sawdust on the floor, bakers, greengrocers, with a general store for other food and house wares. Very few items were ready packed, so biscuits, for example, would have to be taken from a large tin, placed in a paper bag and weighed to the desired half-pound, adding and taking away a final biscuit until the scales balanced. Sweets, vegetables, bacon, cheese, fruit – everything would be cut, measured and weighed to order, a service that is now available only in specialist shops at a premium price. In the Co-operative store in Immingham, to where the family moved in 1951, daily purchases were listed in a small notebook, along with the price, and once a week, following pay day, the account would be settled, after being deftly totted up by a cashier who added pounds, shillings and pence in one operation (not, as most people did, starting with the pence, followed by the shillings and ending with the pounds).

A shopping trip for groceries could take an hour or more, and the purchases would have to be carried home in your own shopping bags (no free plastic bags in those days), on foot or precariously balanced on the handlebars of a bike. Milk came by cart, and later was delivered in bottles that clinked and jangled cheerfully in the early morning. Specialist tradesmen delivered bread, fish, meat or greengroceries once, twice or three times a week, initially by horse-drawn cart, later in motorised vans, making life easier for housewives like my mother.

That particular cottage in Barnetby, to which my parents moved in late 1948, was their first real home after living for six or seven years of marriage in one or two rented rooms. My father transferred to the railway depot at Barnetby after the war, and they initially rented two ground-floor rooms of Number 9, Silver Street. The street consisted of small semis, with narrow alleys between the pairs. At the back of the house was a coal shed, built in brick and attached to the house. In those days, coal was roughly hewn from the mine and delivered by the sack load in enormous chunks to individual houses, where the inhabitants had to use a large hammer to break the fuel to a size that the grate could accommodate. Many is the morning or afternoon I sat in the coal-shed wielding a hammer at a large block of coal. 'I'm conking,' I proudly told our neighbour, Mrs Winterbottom, as she passed by one day. To me, aged three and a half, 'conking' seemed the most natural pastime in the world, more engaging than my toys.

Not that there were many toys to be had in post-war Britain. I do recall, though, my fourth birthday present: a Hornby train set comprising a green engine and coal tender, clockwork-operated, that ran round and round a circular track pulling one or two goods wagons. It probably cost one pound, and my mother would have paid for it at a shilling a week for twenty weeks in Vickers's shop at the end of the street on Victoria Road.

My brother later acquired a similar model in red, with passenger coaches. I was extremely happy with it, until we moved later in the year and I discovered that the Pratt kids next door had a similar toy but with one important feature: a lever that could allow the thing to drive *backwards* as well as forwards. Small boys' envy arrives fully grown. Over the next few years, John and I acquired more carriages and wagons, rails, points, buffers, signals and other fittings for our combined train set, including gifts from cousins who had outgrown their own. These kept us occupied indoors on wet afternoons, until other interests took over.

The move from two rented rooms to a whole rented cottage was a matter of half a mile, and there were not many items of furniture, clothing or other belongings to be transported. A full-scale removal van was quite unnecessary, so my father hired the services of Mr Fowler, the local greengrocer, whose black horse-drawn cart served the purpose admirably. The move was completed in half an evening. Dad told me years later that, following the move into their first complete home, he and my mother felt as though they owned the earth.

It was certainly no palace. Four rooms – two up and two downstairs. The only entrance was through the back door, into the kitchen with its built-in copper for heating water, drawn by the bucketful from the communal pump. A couple of years after we moved in, a single tap on a stand pipe was installed in the yard to bring a source of treated water for the four dwellings. The electrical supply was very basic: a single light in the centre of each room, and a few sockets for the sparse number of electrically operated gadgets that we possessed.

These included – in fact, were little more than – an elderly bakelite radio that for many years served as a source of information for my parents and of family entertainment. A lunchtime ritual when John and I were toddlers was to sit in rapt attention and 'Listen with Mother' to the nursery rhymes and daily story read by Daphne Oxenford, always preceded by the formula: 'Are you sitting comfortably? Then I'll begin.' There we first became familiar with 'Sing a Song of Sixpence', and the story of the little engine that struggled to pull a train up an incline ('I think I can, I think I can' to the rhythm of the track) and down the other side of the hill ('I knew I could, I knew I could'). Our learning was reinforced in the illustrated books that came as birthday or Christmas presents. My first book, for my sixth birthday, was *Our Feathered Friends*, an illustrated book of birds with an embossed full-colour robin on the cover.

In the kitchen my mother did much of the cooking on a paraffin-fuelled Primus stove, later supplemented by a second. For sheer convenience and as a means of cost saving, she discovered the joys and woes of the pressure cooker: joys because cooking times and paraffin consumption were significantly reduced; woes because in her hands everything was grossly overcooked – potatoes and cabbage were treated identically, along with carrots, Brussels sprouts and all other vegetables.

Straight ahead from the back door was the entrance to the parlour (although that word was not in our vocabulary: we called it 'the front room'), which had a cast-iron fireplace with an integrated oven for baking or for roasting the Sunday joint. This was the main heating in the house, and was lit most days of the year – much like the Aga or Rayburn ranges in modern rural dwellings.

The front room was where we spent most of our daytime hours. It was fairly sparsely furnished: a table in the centre, with a plain wooden top and two extending leaves. My mother would scrub this regularly. There was a couch with a couple of easy chairs; a sideboard and four matching dining chairs stained dark brown, almost black, all bought second-hand and at one stage taken away for stripping and French polishing in a mid-oak shade – these stayed in my parents' possession for all their married life; and a few other bits and pieces. Another table, a polished drop-leaf model, appeared within a year or so – bought new, which was unusual. Linoleum covered the floor, and in front of the fire a rug, made by Dad from 'snips': strips of old knitwear about four inches by one inch, roughly sorted by colour, and threaded using a special hook into a sheet of hessian to make a simple pattern.

There was no bathroom (since there was no water supply), so basic washing was done in the kitchen. Each evening, my mother would heat water and half-fill an oval enamel bowl, place this on the table in the front room, and stand me and then my brother in it to give us a thorough washing down. Once a week, the copper would be heated and the water transferred by bucket into a large oval galvanised bath on the rug before the fire, and my brother and I would be bathed in turn (using the same water, of course). I was not aware of it at the time, but I imagine my parents did the same after we boys had been put to bed.

Immediately to the left of the entrance door was another door flush with the wall and about eight inches from the floor: the height of the first stair to the upper floor. Ten steps brought us to a tiny landing. Turn right and through a door, down three steps into the room over the kitchen, designated my bedroom, although I think my brother also slept there on a smaller bed. From that room I was carried by ambulance crew in November 1949 for a spell in hospital. As I was carried out of the house, wrapped in a hospital blanket, I saw the figure of a public health official, waiting to light a disinfecting candle in my room.

At the top of the stairs, our parents' room was straight ahead, down three steps, to the front of the house. A double wardrobe stood on the wall to the left, and the marital bed took up the centre of the room. There was a small cast-iron fireplace to the right, sharing the chimney stack with the fireplace in the front room. A dressing table and a painted wicker chair completed the sparse furnishings. This was the bedroom in which my brother suffered his measles, with the curtains closed. I went through mumps and chicken pox in the same room. And one Christmas Eve, while Dad was at work and my mother toiled downstairs preparing mince pies, jam tarts and other party fare, I was in the same bedroom, failing to fall asleep as I excitedly awaited the arrival of Santa Claus (to reduce the level of excitement, John and I were separated for that night). Dad came home from work shortly before midnight and desperately sneaked the Christmas stocking upstairs – to his dismay, because I discovered it and wondered how on earth Santa could have delivered it without my being aware. Dad denied having met him on the stairs, and this puzzle was the start of my disbelief.

In the absence of a bathroom, the toilet was outside. The two end cottages each had their own privy, built into their individual block of outhouses, which also contained a coal shed and a pig-sty. The two central cottages had a separate block of privies. Their doors faced away from the cottages, and a simple boxed-in wooden seat covered the receptacle that was emptied weekly and disposed of by council workers. In winter, we would carry a candle inside a jar across the yard to do our business. In order to clamber on to the seat, I would carry what I thought of as my grandfather's stool – a wooden footstool that has been in the family since well before I was born.

The privy became a source of amusement to my brother and myself. Our neighbours to the left, the Pratt family, had three children: Ann, John and Tommy, who was just a titch when their father was killed in a cycling accident on his way home from work. While undoubtedly toilet-trained, Tommy had not yet learnt to button his trousers and so needed assistance after visits across the yard. On many occasions we would watch with amusement from our kitchen window as Tommy peeped round the corner of the privy, saw that the coast was clear, and dashed to their door, trousers in hand.

Although each cottage had a pig-sty, only one family kept pigs: the Carlines, at Number 1, and then on their garden plot rather than in the designated sty. Once a year, the squealing pigs were taken off to be slaughtered, and on the following day the communal yard witnessed the scene of carving up a carcass, much as generations had done right across Europe. My father used our sty to keep bikes, tools, bits of timber and various junk that he couldn't face throwing out.

It was in our pig-sty that I first had doubts about my father's technical competence. I was six or seven. In the years of post-war shortages, supplies of many goods and products were irregular. Items would appear in a village shop, immediately attract attention and be snapped up. Families who were too slow, or simply couldn't afford it, had to do without. When the Pratt and Carline children were given sunglasses, my brother and I felt deprived, but my mother's weekly budget did not stretch to such an unnecessary luxury for John and me. So she cut out cardboard frames and inserted garish yellow cellophane, which convinced us for a couple of hours, although I was disappointed to discover that they didn't permit me to look directly at the sun. When the Pratt boys were given toy guns and percussion caps, so that they could play cowboys and Indians with some degree of conviction, I again expressed my sense of deprivation to my father. In response he took me to the pig-sty, picked up a hammer and a couple of nails, and fastened together two pieces of wood, one for the handle, the other representing the barrel of the gun. So disgusted was I at this crude effort that I refused to play with it – and I had very little confidence in Dad's manual skills after that.

To the rear of the row of cottages, beyond the common yard with its pig-sties, its water pump and later standpipe with a communal tap, and its privy block, there were four sizeable plots for growing vegetables, fruit and flowers. We had a couple of apple trees, and my parents planted blackcurrant bushes and raspberry canes. The apples were not particularly tasty, and did not cook well, but we ate them anyway. The blackcurrants and raspberries were prolific, and were picked each year and baked in pies, conserved in Kilner jars for the coming year, or turned into jam. In addition, my father grew an array of vegetables: radishes, lettuce, potatoes, carrots, peas, runner beans, broad beans, beetroot (which my mother alone in the family ate), sometimes onions.

Dad was a fantastic digger, energetic and methodical. He would set out his line of string, which he wound on to a flattened iron bobbin that spun round a central spindle, its other end attached to an iron stake. The line in place as a guide, held by the iron stakes at each side of the plot, he would dig rhythmically across the garden, pause to move the line back nine inches or a foot, and continue, all the while singing quietly to himself – mainly hymns which, as a Methodist, he had grown up with. The line was also used for making straight seed rows with the back of a rake. Dad seemed happiest when engaging in such activity. It made few mental demands on him; he needed no special dexterity, which suited him fine; he could avoid the carping criticism that greeted any attempts to do 'practical' things with his hands; and the garden produce eased the family budget immeasurably. My mother would help with the sowing and the harvesting, devoting a whole summer afternoon to picking raspberries or blackcurrants, and then the whole evening or the following day to making jam or bottling the fruit. When we moved to Immingham Dad took on an allotment in addition to our garden and grew many of our own vegetables.

On Tuesday mornings, the washing line would be extended along one side of the garden path, and my mother would spend her day getting up early to light the fire under the copper to heat the water, then washing bed-linen and clothes in the kitchen, carrying them out and pegging them to the line, continuing with the washing indoors, bringing in the dry items and replacing them with more clothes, freshly boiled, washed, squeezed, rinsed and squeezed again. It was an exhausting life. It must have left my mother quite drained, but we rarely heard her complain.

The Pratts didn't use their garden plot after the death of the head of the family. Instead, we children used to use it for play. From the garden we had a superb view of the railway line that extended inland from the mouth of the Humber at Grimsby and Cleethorpes. At Barnetby the railway line from the coast splits into three, heading towards Scunthorpe and Doncaster and beyond in a northerly and westerly direction – Wakefield and Leeds, Sheffield, Manchester and eventually Liverpool; the next leads towards Gainsborough and thence to the East Coast main line at Retford; the third runs south to Lincoln, and then southwest to Newark, Leicester and Birmingham. The weekly cattle market in the village was located adjacent to the railway station, and trains were used to ferry the livestock from farm to market and from market to processing factory.

Apart from passenger traffic to points east and west, all manner of goods and freight passed through the station, heading to and from the ports of Immingham and Grimsby. Periodically in the racing season one could see on the station platform piles of wicker baskets containing pigeons, on their way to remote locations for release at a specified time. Once a year, in summer, a special train would be hired for a Church Sunday School outing from Barnetby to the resort of Cleethorpes, less than an hour away, where we would enjoy building sandcastles, paddling in the sea, taking rides on donkeys on the beach or on the miniature railway, or getting rid of pennies – and occasionally winning prizes – in the slot machines of Wonderland. Sometimes the annual trip was to a more distant resort: I was confined to bed with chicken pox in the year they went to Scarborough.

A regular train of particular interest that passed through Barnetby was the daily fish express from Grimsby, carrying much of the morning's catch to Billingsgate in London. Frequently, Dad would be working as a fireman on the engine of this train, earning his seven or eight pounds a week in return for shovelling tons of coal into the firebox over a decade or more, until promotion led him to drive the engine. Many is the Easter and summer holiday morning when we children would be in the garden at the time the train passed by. Dad would ask the driver to give an unauthorised whistle as the train approached, and he would wave at us as they sped by. I think the neighbours' children were impressed.

Long before this stage, though, I was well into my primary school, in the class of Miss Freeston, my first teacher, loved by generations of primary school pupils in St Barnabas' primary school in Barnetby until her retirement in the mid-1950s.

3

St. Barnabas' Primary School

'What time is it, Mister Wolf?'
- 'One o'clock'
- 'What time is it, Mister Wolf?'
- 'Three o'clock'
- 'What time is it, Mister Wolf?'
- 'Ten o'clock'
- 'What time is it, Mister Wolf?'
- 'My dinner time – Grrrrrrr!'

and a dozen five-year-olds would run away from their teacher in feigned terror. This little game was repeated a couple of times more along the lane at the back of the school, until we reached the main road and skipped off on our separate ways. We children loved our teacher, Miss Freeston.

On my first day at school, in September 1948, I said a nervous 'good-bye' to my mother, went through the school doors and turned left, past the coat racks to the immediate left of the door, and into Miss Freeston's classroom. She seemed very, very old, although she cannot have been much over sixty, if that. She reminded me of 'Auntie Sanders', the elderly lady whom we used to visit in Sheffield, but with a *joie de vivre* in the company of small children that my childless adoptive aunt lacked. She too was small, her body bent forward, her silver hair likewise tied back in a bun, and she wore similar round glasses. But her jaw did not tremble – probably because she was a decade younger than 'Auntie Sanders' – and her warm smile reflected an undisguised affection towards her little charges, probably twenty or so in the class. We sat at desks designed for two, in rows, and Miss Freeston stood at the front beside a blackboard on an easel and boxes of chalks, white and coloured. In these disciplined ranks we learned our arithmetical tables and our ABC, and first held a pencil to form the letters of the alphabet. We played games, and were awarded gold and silver stars for our homework. I don't remember being particularly talented in any field, but I suppose I coped, and I got on well enough with the other boys and girls in the class. My early exercise books don't reveal signs of genius. As Christmas approached, we all made paper chains for use as decorations at home, and I'm sure my mother held on to these and used them for two or three years after we first brought them home. Then there was singing. We practised Christmas carols as the autumn progressed, and as with every generation of infants, our lungs were not big enough to allow us to get through a line without a loud intake of breath:

> Away in a [BREATH] manger
> No crib for a [BREATH] bed [BREATH]
> The little [BREATH] Lord Jesus
> Lay [BREATH] down his sweet [BREATH] head ...

And there was the world's most famous nursery rhyme, on which Mozart famously composed a set of variations, best known in the English-speaking world as 'Twinkle, Twinkle, Little Star'. In Miss Freeston's class we sang different words:

> Little Arabella Miller found a woolly caterpillar.
> First it crawled upon her mother
> Then upon her baby brother.
> All said, 'Arabella Miller, take away that caterpillar!'

But for one boy in the class – I think his name was Graham – this was a bit too complicated. He couldn't pronounce the letter 'l': it came out as 'r', which was bad enough. On top of that, he was thrown into confusion by the elimination from the last line of one of the adjectives that appeared in the first. Graham's version, when he was asked to perform the song solo, came out as:

> Littre Araberra Mirrer found a woorry caterpirrar.
> First it crawred upon her mother

Then upon her baby brother.
Arr said, 'Araberra Mirrer, take away that woorry cater...'

He stopped as he realised that the line wouldn't scan. He tried again:

Arr said, 'Littre Araberra Mirrer ...'

And he collapsed in tears, as the rest of the class laughed at his attempts. Children are so cruel.

In the second class, pupils from two separate years would be combined for an hour's singing with the headmaster, Mr Clark ('Nobby', of course, to everyone), in what passed for the school hall – two classrooms that could be combined by folding back a wall of wooden panels that separated them. One Wednesday afternoon, as the rain poured down outside, Mr Clark was drilling us in the round, 'London's Burning':

London's burning, London's burning –
Look yonder, look yonder.
Fire, Fire! Fire, Fire!
Go get me some water.

Even six-year-olds were amused by the thought of a call for water, given the lashing on the windows. Mr Clark looked out, pointed through the window, and launched into a solo:

It's raining, it's raining –
Look yonder, look yonder.
Rain, rain! Rain, rain!
Just look at that water.

In that school hall, too, I had my first experience of participating in a public performance. It was the Christmas Nativity play, in which I was designated one of the three 'Kings' – a convenient interpretation of the 'wise men' of the Bible since it has allowed generations of five-year-olds simply to don a paper crown and a sheet to play the part. My single line was straightforward, but I agonised over it. In the stable in Bethlehem, another of the 'Kings' announced that we had come from Herod's palace. That was my cue. I turned towards 'Joseph', inclined my body slightly in his direction, and uttered my well-rehearsed explanation: 'We thought we might find Him there.'

In the audience, my parents, I'm sure, were immensely proud – but this did not presage a career on the stage, for which I would have been given little encouragement. My mother participated keenly in amateur dramatics in the Women's Institute, where she also convincingly performed some of Joyce Grenfell's and other authors' monologues, continuing a skill for which she had been awarded prizes in school. From her I learned something about stage make-up, and tricks such as using a sticking plaster to cover a wedding ring when playing the character of an unmarried girl: I appreciated that it would not be seen by the audience. But the theatre as entertainment was never a part of our lives. Rather, the professional theatre was remote, expensive and middle-class, and hence of little interest to my father in particular.

Miss Freeston had infinite patience, which must have been tested when a Down's syndrome child joined the class. In the 1940s that was a bold experiment, but it was not entirely successful. The poor child, Michael, communicated very poorly, and to make matters very difficult, he was incontinent. Day after day, Miss Freeston would be obliged to clean him, and throw sand on the classroom floor. Among the emotions evoked in the minds of us six-year-olds, I think embarrassment predominated. After a few weeks Michael was withdrawn.

Sometimes on my way home I would call into the little bakehouse behind Kirkby's general store on the corner of Victoria Road and Silver Street, where my Uncle Bill worked as a baker. I was always fascinated by the long wooden troughs in which he would mix the flour, yeast, salt and water into dough, the oven and the wooden paddles that he used for placing tins of unbaked dough into the oven and removing the warm, crispy loaves and rolls. Sometimes he would have a tiny ball of dough left over that he had put into the oven, and if I were lucky he would give it to me, still warm, to take home for tea. One day I called in to discover a new piece of equipment in the corner: a gigantic stainless-steel electric mixer, into which he would add the ingredients of bread, by the sackful, and switch on the machine to save time and effort in mixing by hand. This was a sign of progress, and perhaps an attempt to compete with the bigger bakeries in Grimsby, the largest nearby town. It ultimately failed, though. The Kirkby family could not afford to give Uncle Bill a pay rise, so he resigned, found a job in the steelworks in Scunthorpe, moved to that town, and Barnetby lost its village bakery, in a pattern that was repeated across the country.

In my teens, I briefly helped a baker in Immingham with a bread delivery round in local villages. But that establishment, too, could not survive the competition of large-scale bakeries owned by big milling companies. In the 1970s, I saw the same story played out in a German film, *Das Brot des Bäckers* (The Baker's Bread), where a village baker, who obviously adored his craft, was undercut by a bigger company, sent his sons to buy rolls in bulk from the local supermarket and then sold them as his own, and was ultimately reduced to mechanically lifting trays of shaped dough into the oven and removing them after the prescribed time to supply the village with a standardised product.

Life in those post-war years was certainly primitive in comparison with today's existence in most of England. Not only were families lacking in possessions and suffering from an acute housing shortage, but the basic amenities that nowadays we take for granted had simply never reached small villages. Sanitary arrangements were very basic. The village bakery was, in a sense, a mixed blessing: bread was fresh, hand-crafted and wholesome; but the variety was limited. Milk was delivered, unpasteurised, by horse and trap by the farmer, who would ladle it into jugs at the door, using a pint or half-pint dipping measure. Refrigerators came into common use only in the 1960s, so keeping food fresh was a constant problem in warm weather. Meat was bought directly from the butcher. In the late 1940s, a knife-sharpener would travel from village to village offering his services, which he carried out using an abrasive circular stone attached by a driving belt to the pedals of his bicycle. Shoe repairs were performed by the village cobbler, or through house-to-house collection and delivery by a representative from a nearby town. Fruit and vegetables likewise were delivered to the door by Mr Fowler, whose horse-drawn trailer we used in the move to our cottage.

In those years, Gypsies came round periodically, selling the fruits of their winter labours: carved wooden chrysanthemums, or clothes pegs. Exotic tradesmen from India hawked 'silk' ties, carried in suitcases from door to door. Occasionally a tramp would call, begging. I remember one who held an egg to show my mother through our kitchen window: it had been given by a neighbour, and my mother invited him in, boiled it for him, and tried to dry his wet overcoat as he sat at our scullery table and ate it with bread and butter and a mug of tea.

Cars were a pretty uncommon sight in the village, so walking and cycling posed little danger, at least in daylight. My father would normally travel to work on his bike – and for railwaymen such as him on night or early morning duty, a 'knocker-up' would call at the house to make sure he was awake in good time for his shift. There was no assumption that every railwayman's household possessed an alarm clock.

John and I were about six and seven when we acquired our first set of two wheels, replacing the little tricycles that we had used until then. My bike – second- or even third-hand, of course, and refurbished by a local mechanic: nothing as expensive as a bicycle could be afforded new – was slightly too big for me, and I had wooden blocks attached to the pedals for a few months until I grew to fit the frame. We boys were photographed by our father, using his Kodak box camera, wearing our best clothes, complete with little peaked caps, ties, knee-length socks and polished shoes, and in my case a sign of pure vanity: a large comb protruding from the breast pocket. These bikes were the epitome of our schoolboy pride, and we soon learned to ride them. We could now go with Dad to visit members of his family in nearby villages – until one occasion, when my attention was distracted by a rabbit at the side of the road. I swerved, lost my balance, and fell off, damaging the bike, which had to be left at our destination for repair.

John's first bike had tiny wheels, yet in 1952 he followed the road signs from Immingham to Barnetby, an adventure that would be far too dangerous today (and was pretty risky in those days). My mother marvelled at the number of times his feet would have gone round on the pedals on a journey of sixteen miles or so to visit Auntie Florrie. After refreshment, and a phone call to a neighbour, he was put on a train to Habrough, where he was met and accompanied on the three-mile journey home.

It was in that atmosphere of relative deprivation that I encountered politics for the first time. On 23 February 1950, after a term in which a Labour government had taken the steel industry, the railways, road transport and other basic sectors under state control and established the National Health Service, a fresh election led to a new Labour government with a much-diminished majority. The details meant nothing to me, at the age of six and a half, but I remember the 'battle bus' of the re-elected MP for Brigg, Lance Mallalieu, passing down the King's Road in Barnetby on his victory tour of the constituency. It can hardly be said that my future career as a political scientist was sparked by that event, but it certainly made an impression on me.

So did, three years later, the death of the Soviet dictator, Joseph Stalin. We were on holiday, staying with my Uncle Arthur and his family (my mother's second brother). Arthur, blind from his teenage years, worked in the Ministry of Labour, and travelled daily by Tube into central London. He had been the first blind person to pass the intermediate examination of the National Association of Local Government Officers, in 1934, when he worked as a clerk for Lindsey County Council. After moving to London and living in the village of Oxhey, near Watford, an early task had been to count and memorise the clickety-clicks between stations on the Bakerloo Line: then, if he happened to fall asleep, he could count the clicks between the next two stations – they varied by quite a few thousand – and would know where he was. That trick, and others, gave him a measure of independence that was truly impressive. He became passionate about hi-fi in later years, and invented a modified cassette tape recorder for use by blind students, after his daughter, my cousin Margaret, also blind, completed a degree in history at Leicester University. In March 1953, on a day visit to London from Oxhey, we saw the newspaper headlines announcing Stalin's death. My parents commented, and explained to me in simple terms who he had been. I can certainly date my awareness of the Soviet Union from then but, again, it meant little to me at the time. The idea of a career as a Kremlinologist was far, far beyond the horizon – the very word took a decade to enter my consciousness.

I was a studious child, quite unlike my brother, who was rarely indoors. Far more happy-go-lucky than I ever was (perhaps I suffered from the 'first child' syndrome), he would be out in the garden playing with the other children – the Carlines and the Pratts from our yard, kids from up the street, others who might turn up from elsewhere in the village. They would contentedly run around for hours, playing I don't (and didn't) know what games. Cowboys and Indians? Football? Tag? Climbing the apple trees? Perhaps all of these. Occasionally I joined in, but for most of the time I was quite indifferent. I would stay indoors, sitting by the fire-place in our front room, with my notebooks and pencils, doodling, reading, writing, drawing. I don't remember anything as being particularly inspired. It was certainly not the creative stirring of a future man of letters, mathematician or artist. But it kept me quiet and occupied at least.

My first school exercise books – lovingly retained by my mother – reveal some of my academic strengths and weaknesses, and also some of the values we post-war children were expected to absorb. Particular attention seems to have been paid to handwriting. Miss Freeston's comments included 'poor writing' on more than one page, and my pencil drawings bore scant resemblance to what they represented. Yet I spent hours indoors, amusing myself with pencil and paper.

In school, at the age of eight, I demonstrated my feet-on-the-ground, no-nonsense, logical mind, in my analysis of the story of Goldilocks and the three bears. My English exercise on Thursday, 15 March 1951 read as follows:

> Do you know the story of "The Three Bears?" It is the best story about bears. Of course, it is not true. It is just a story. Bears do not live in houses. They do not have beds like ours. They do not have chairs. They do not talk as we do.

A few months later, I tried my hand at verse (I shrink from calling it poetry):

My Garden

Oh, in my garden every day
It should be always playtime,
And every bird should have a nest,
And all the world be Maytime!

And everywhere would be my own,
And there would grow together
White winter flowers and buttercups,
All in sunny weather.

I must have benefited from practising handwriting, because a couple of years later I entered a children's competition run by *Good Housekeeping* magazine. The task was to complete the rhyming couplet, 'Roses are red, violets are blue'. I have no recollection of how I completed the rhyme, but a few weeks later I received a postal order for half a crown (two shillings and sixpence, or 12.5p), the third prize. When in its next issue the magazine announced the results, Ronald Hill was commended for his 'bold hand'.

My grasp of arithmetic seems to have been a little more secure. The pages of the little exercise books – made, in those cash-starved years, by the teacher, who cut the paper, folded it, and stitched the leaves together with a needle and thread – are smothered with equations, corrected with blue or sometimes red pencil ticks and the occasional cross for an error. A page of divisions ($2 \div 2 = 1$; $4 \div 2 = 2$; $9 \div 3 = 3$ down to $14 \div 2 = 7$) is followed by multiplication ($1 \times 4 = 4$ . . . $7 \times 4 = 28$...) with a silver star affixed by Miss Freeston and 'Good' in her clear royal blue hand. The final page in this second set of mathematics exercises introduced me and the class to currency, at a time of pounds, shillings, pence – £.s.d. – and even ha'pennies and farthings, on the verge of joining the groat – fourpence – and the guinea (one pound and one shilling) forever in the historical past of Britain's coinage. A row of six little circles followed by what looked like a semi-circle was how I counted 6½ pence (just over 2.5 pence in today's decimal currency).

We were also shown samples of the coins, or at least cardboard replicas and coloured pictures in our textbooks, to familiarise ourselves and prepare for the world of trade: the shilling, or 'bob', twenty to the pound; the florin, or two-bob bit; the half-crown, worth two shillings and sixpence, and also colloquially known as a half-dollar (or half a dollar), since that was its approximate value during the war; the shy little six-penny coin, known as the 'tanner' (of which forty made a pound); the twelve-sided threepenny bit, of a brass-coloured alloy, with a thrift flower on the obverse (an old silver threepenny bit was a rarity by then, but occasionally they turned up in a Christmas pudding); the large copper penny, twelve to the shilling, that weighed heavily in the pocket or purse (in the 1940s there were still plenty of 'bun pennies' in circulation – coins that had survived since the young Queen Victoria, whose image on the 'head' side depicted her wearing a bun hair style); the ha'penny, and the farthing (fourthing, or quarter-penny), with the cute image of a wren that appealed to us children. I imagine it was a difficult task to teach this ancient and irrational system of currency to children, and teachers must have greeted as a salvation the transfer to decimal coinage in February 1971, even though it contained a tiny half-penny coin that was valued at more than the massive old penny and has long ceased to circulate.

Possibly as a result of this focused activity, I was believed to be suffering from eye strain, so I was taken to an optician in Grimsby, twenty miles or so away. The drops inserted to open my pupils were not treated with an antidote at the end of the eye examination, in order, so I was told, to give my eyes a rest, and I suffered blurred vision for several hours until the effect of the drops wore off. A week or so later I received my first glasses: round functional frames, and practical arms that clipped over the ears – nowadays considered a classic design. I thought them distinctly 'uncool' – although that was a term that did not come into vogue until five decades or so later. I was embarrassed as I put them on for the first time in class, and was relieved when after a year or so I was told I no longer needed them.

I still preferred to be indoors to playing outside with my brother and our neighbours' children. This continued to provoke feelings of anxiety in my mother, who no doubt discussed it with the neighbours and perhaps her sisters, whose own children were several years ahead of John and me in our life-path.

'Bairns need fresh air' was the received wisdom – and so they do. 'A child should be running around' – and exercise is certainly a Good Thing. 'He's growing pasty-faced' – unlike other children and my brother with the 'roses' in their cheeks. All this reading and writing would cause eye-strain: hadn't I, after all, been prescribed glasses for my eyes?

It was determined that the family doctor should be consulted, so I was dragged along to his surgery and examined. There was evidently nothing physically ailing me at that stage (my brother and I had long recovered from whooping cough; German measles, mumps, chicken pox and scarlet fever came later), but the doctor agreed that spending hours indoors was Not Good For Me. Neither, of course, was it good for my mother to have a small child in the house, tied to her apron strings, when she was trying to clean, cook, prepare a fire, or tackle a mountain of ironing after a Tuesday morning's washing. The doctor's advice was uncompromising: 'Lock him out!' – and it sounded more like an order.

So my mother, always willing to bend to the authority of an expert, obeyed. On the following morning, with the sun shining brightly, and my brother and the Pratt children happily running about the yard and garden, I was placed outside the back door and instructed to go and play; the door was securely locked.

I had no notion of complying. Without sobbing or crying, or even whining, I waited by the door. And continued to wait. I explained to the curious Mrs Jenkins, our neighbour, that I had been locked out, and she sympathised, with a knowing smile. After a quarter of an hour or so, my mother opened the door and put her head out to enquire about my condition. I had not moved. And I still had no interest in playing. I continued to wait. After an hour or so my mother conceded defeat, invited me indoors, and let me return to my solitary pursuits.

The experiment was never repeated, so far as I recall. I was essentially bookish, not the outdoor type, and the family grew to live with the fact.

Sometimes, though, I did join in the outdoor activities. Just up the hill, beyond the Railway Inn, there is a lovely old house which used to have a large garden to the rear (to small boys, at any rate, the garden seemed huge). The place was owned by Mr Havercroft, known to everyone as 'Cockerel', but as a boy I never knew why. Only on a visit to the village sixty years later did I learn that it was because his voice had not properly broken in adolescence, so occasionally in mid-word he would break into a falsetto, rather like a cock crowing. He lived alone in what we assumed was a rambling Victorian house, and in the summer, as he tended his garden, with its monkey-puzzle tree and pampas grass, its fruit trees, its bean rows and a variety of other vegetables and bushes, he would wear a straw hat, which, together with his luxuriant moustache, completed the image of an amiable but formidable figure.

We children – or, at least, the boys from the neighbourhood – would frequently use his garden for play, walking impudently into his potting shed and running along the pathways that separated the various plots. Along one side there was a brick wall with a door that led to an orchard, through which we were occasionally allowed to venture. It was rather like the door in the children's novel *The Secret Garden*, leading to a world that was normally closed to us little interlopers. In fact, when we became a bit too boisterous the whole garden was deemed out of bounds, and we were chased out and had to find other places to play – as often as not our own back yards, which had none of the magical attraction of Cockerel Havercroft's garden.

Boys and girls usually played separately, of course: girls had dolls and skipping ropes, and chanted rhythmic nonsense songs as they skipped; boys kicked balls outdoors and played with train sets inside. But we were certainly aware of the opposite sex, and sometimes played in groups together. We chased each other in games of 'tag', and occasionally the girls were allowed to join in an improvised game of cricket, with the 'stumps' drawn in chalk on an outhouse wall. Sometimes we pretended to be doctors and nurses (with the stereotyped division of roles), although what we actually *did* in playing such roles has escaped my memory.

Although much of our activity outside school was voluntarily segregated, boys and girls shared classes in school, sometimes experienced longings for others, and ascribed to individuals 'relationships' that had no substance. 'Boyfriends' and 'girlfriends' were not serious concepts, but the terms were thrown casually about. I was told that my 'girlfriend' was our neighbour, Ann Pratt – yet there was no emotional connection between us.

Even so, I early became a sucker for a pretty face. Almost from the start of my primary school career, I had been very sweet on a blonde named Gillian, but I was far too shy to speak to her, so she never had an inkling of my admiration. I was, by my mother's account decades later, quite a little gentleman, helping the girls to put on their coats before going home from school, but I was certainly not precocious in my relations with the opposite sex. Gillian's allure surpassed that of all others. When we moved up to the next class, Miss Beverly's, there was an uneven balance of boys and girls, and since the desks were designed for two pupils one boy had to share a desk with one girl. I was beside myself when I proved to be the 'odd' boy and was allotted the seat next to Gillian! Oh, the blissful agony that I suffered for a term, before my family moved away and I lost all contact with my innocent beloved. I had also had an infantile fancy for another six-year-old, Doreen, dark haired, unlike Gillian, but equally pretty, and – unusually in the late 1940s – she and her elder sister Maureen wore trousers to school. I worshipped silently from a distance.

One thing I did enjoy out of doors was walking up the hill to a nearby wood – Gallows Wood (standing opposite a seventeenth-century gibbet) – to climb trees or simply wander among the bluebells, campions and ragged robins. Our neighbour Mrs Jenkins frequently used to walk there with a little cloth bag to pick up sticks for kindling, and she regularly invited the children to accompany her and her white Scottie dog, Terry. When this activity had become essentially routine, children would see Mrs Jenkins with her coat, headscarf and walking shoes or Wellingtons, and carrying her bag, and invite themselves along. She had no children of her own, but we in the neighbourhood served as substitute family. Alas, I was far too shy. Mrs Jenkins would appear, suitably attired for a walk to Gallows Wood to go 'sticking', and the other children would cheerfully ask to accompany her. 'Can we come with you, Mrs Jenkins?', to which she always readily agreed. But I stood aloof, waiting – desperately wanting to be invited, but too timid to say so. She would spot me, smile in my direction, say something along the lines of 'Ronald is always too shy to ask', and invite me to join them. I would happily tag along.

A dozen years or more after we left the village, I returned on a visit out of curiosity. I had just graduated from Leeds University by that stage, so I was rather different in appearance from the eight-year-old who had last lived in 3 Grey Cottages. I hesitantly approached the door to Number 4, and knocked. Mrs Jenkins answered, looking a little plumper than I remembered, which was probably natural: she once said to my mother: 'After the change of life, either you go fat or you go scrawny. I reckon you're going to go scrawny.' This was Northern directness at its most direct. Why call a spade a spade when you can call it a bloody shovel?

'I bet you don't remember me!', I offered. She studied my face quizzically for a couple of moments. 'I bet I do!' – and so she did, and she invited me in for tea and cake. Her husband John came in from the garden, by then wearing a hearing aid. He had no memory of me, although he certainly remembered my parents. 'Mr and Mrs Jenks', as my father called them, had bought their cottage when the block had been put up for sale, and they were the only family still living there.

Even later, in my sixties, I was curious to see my old haunts, so on a visit to my mother in Scunthorpe I flew to Humberside airport and took a taxi to the village. The four cottages were still there, now with bathrooms, running water and a decent electricity supply. Mr and Mrs Jenkins had long gone, but Numbers 1 and 2 had been bought by the former owners of the Railway Inn, on the adjacent plot, and converted into a single dwelling. When I introduced myself and explained my association with the place, they immediately recalled how my father had helped them move into the Inn more than half a century earlier. Number 3, our house, was now inhabited by a centenarian, living alone, still very lucid - and very surprised when I knocked on the door.

Apart from the row of cottages, there was little left to remind me of my boyhood activities and haunts. The four garden plots were untended, and the malt kiln that dominated the view from our back garden - where we had played together with the Pratt children, the Carlines and others - was abandoned and awaiting demolition. The Railway Inn still stands, as does Cockerel Havercroft's house; but the 'secret' orchard long ago became a housing estate. Much building has taken place at the other end of the village, near to the school that I attended from September 1948 until December 1951.

In the middle of my time in St. Barnabas' school, in November 1949, along with a number of other children in the village I was diagnosed with scarlet fever. It turned out that my brother had carried it home, during his first term at school, although he didn't develop the illness. Once the disease was confirmed, I was kept in bed for a day, then bundled into a blanket, carried to an ambulance and taken fifteen miles to Brumby Isolation Hospital in Scunthorpe, clutching an empty Horlicks jar containing Cadbury's Buttons - one of the few things I could suck with my sore throat. Alas, on arrival at the hospital they were taken from me and I never saw them again. From my isolation ward I saw the empty jar being removed from a cupboard in the nurses' common room at the end of the week. It was a disenchanting experience.

I knew several of the other children when I was moved to the open ward, but that helped little. I got to know the taste of penicillin, a recent antibiotic that was then taken as a liquid medicine. I also encountered bedpans and 'water bottles' (which I was not good at using, to the dismay of the ward orderlies) and all the rest of the hospital routine - and I am fortunate not to have so far repeated that encounter. I also discovered sago or tapioca pudding - 'frogspawn' pudding, as I thought of it. It may have been sweet and nutritious, but, try as I might, I could not swallow it without retching, and on one occasion I soiled the sheet with my vomiting. It was not the taste, but rather the texture that put me off, and this aversion to slimy, glutinous or rubbery food has remained with me.

Mushrooms, cooked onions, noodles: since 1949 at the latest, I have simply hated the sensation of such dishes in my mouth. Even the jelly inside a pork pie turns my stomach as soon as it reaches my tongue. As for oysters, snails and similar Gallic delicacies.... The other long-term effect of this illness, which entailed my only overnight stay in hospital until more than sixty years later, was a heart murmur that was monitored annually until I left school, by which time it had apparently cleared up.

After a few weeks away from my family, I returned to Barnetby and was devastated to discover that during my absence John had learnt to knit! For an elder brother, this was sheer humiliation. True, the brown woollen gloves that he had managed to create, with help from Mam, were somewhat suggestive of what gloves should be, rather than constituting the real thing. There were multiple dropped stitches, and I doubt whether he ever wore them out of doors. Still, there was the principle of the thing: I had been beaten to a task by my younger sibling! I had to remedy this sign of inferiority. So I too persuaded Mam to teach me the art of making cloth from a ball of wool using a pair of needles.

In fact, I learned pretty quickly, and in subsequent years I went on to great achievements, starting with the patterns that appeared in *Woman* magazine, usually in November with Christmas presents in mind. One year I knitted a guardsman, in bearskin headgear, which was stuffed with kapok and given as a present to my young cousin Margaret. The following year it was a little grey Scottie dog in garter stitch, complete with scarf, a present for another cousin, Sylvia. In later years, as a teenager, I followed patterns to knit at least two sweaters, one of them with an intricate twist in the stitch, which I proudly wore for several years. The tension in the stitches may not have been entirely even, and a decent knitter would have been disappointed with the quality – rather like the produce of an amateur potter, whose cups and bowls are not quite circular or symmetrical. But I was quite pleased with myself, and of course I enjoyed the flattering comments of neighbours and relations.

I also returned from Brumby hospital to hear my mother and brother singing a new Christmas song that was all the rage: 'Rudolph, the Red-Nosed Reindeer', performed on record by 'the singing cowboy' Gene Autrey, and played on the radio. This, too, put my nose out of joint, if only because I could not understand the words: 'You'll go down in history' meant nothing to me. 'Go down where?', I asked my mother, who did her best to explain this idiom to a literal-minded six-year-old.

Conceivably the same year, certainly one December, a new 'musical instrument' appeared in the household: a tin drum, given to my brother as either a Christmas or a birthday present. For an hour or two that morning, John drove my mother scatty with his noisy, unrhythmic bashing: he was not a percussion prodigy, and in later years he took to the electric guitar, with greater success. My mother confiscated the drum, to John's severe dismay, and hid it. He pestered her, but to no avail – until our neighbour Mrs Carline came to his rescue.

'Let the little bugger have it,' she forthrightly advised.

In the face of such blunt instruction, Mam relented. The drum was retrieved from its hiding place in the parental wardrobe, and John was allowed his toy – on condition that he use it exclusively out of doors, ideally at the far end of the garden. (Memo to self: read Günter Grass, *The Tin Drum*, before you die.)

Soon after this episode, my father sensed changes afoot in nationalised British Railways, and applied for a transfer from the Barnetby depot to Immingham. He moved in mid-1950, and for a year and a half travelled the sixteen miles or so to work – by train to Habrough and thence by bike, if the timetables suited, but as often as not biking the whole distance, sometimes during the night, no doubt causing great anxiety to my mother, particularly after the death of our neighbour in a night-time collision with a car. After a year and a half of this regime, the family was allocated a council house at 21 Princess Street, Immingham, to which we moved in December 1951, just in time for Christmas.

That move itself was a memorable occasion, not least because it confirmed my poor opinion of my father and his practicality. A repeat use of Mr Fowler's horse and cart was not possible, since the family now had a few more possessions, and the distance was significant. As a railway employee, Dad was entitled to a concessionary price with the nationalised removals company Pickfords, and arrangements were made to move our modest belongings on 20 December.

There was no sign of a removal van at the appointed time of 9 o'clock, and when 10 came and went, my father was growing anxious. He sent my mother to the nearby Post Office to phone the company (to the end of his life, he was always wary of the telephone and rarely initiated a call). She was assured that we had not been forgotten and the van was on its way, but this did not satisfy Dad, whose impatience led him to carry many of our belongings – the chairs from the three-piece suite, the dining chairs, a dressing table, a wash stand, and tea chests containing sundry items – out of the house, through the yard, and on to the pavement outside. He was quite taken aback when the professionals arrived and did not hide their annoyance at his efforts. They, of course, know how to strip a house and load the van most effectively and efficiently, and my father's misplaced energy had made their life more complicated and even placed obstacles in their way.

I took away another lesson from this: you can learn a lot by observing professionals – even when that professional is your father-in-law. Granddad Wilson was a painter and decorator, and I acquired a number of techniques from watching him; my father, who thought of himself as a dab hand at wallpapering and painting, refused to observe Granddad at work, and struggled to paper round a light switch or avoid streaks in paint, or even use a screw of an appropriate size to fit a toilet roll holder to a bathroom wall. This, too, annoyed my mother, and Dad always felt he was being compared unfavourably with the Wilsons – which indeed he was.

Eventually, in the afternoon five days before Christmas 1951, the van departed, we took the train to Habrough station, completed the journey on our bikes, and the family took up residence in Immingham. Thus began the most formative portion of my life.

4

I.C.E.S.

We arrived at our new home on what remained essentially a building site, with new houses still going up all around. The whole experience must have been tiring for my father and exasperating for my mother, but the move was very exciting to John and me. The new house was far larger than our little two up, two down cottage in Barnetby. It had a proper kitchen, with a gas cooker and a gas copper for boiling the weekly wash. There was a decent-sized sitting room and a separate dining room, and we boys each had our own bedroom. A fireplace in the sitting room even had a back boiler to heat the water, and there was a proper bathroom complete with toilet, and a second toilet downstairs in an outhouse that also included a coal shed and a large shed for bikes, garden tools, wellies, paint cans and anything else. This seemed palatial. But for the first couple of days the great excitement to us was the possibility of running in a circle round the downstairs area: from the sitting room through the dining room into the kitchen, and from there along the hallway back to the sitting room. How we exulted in this freedom! And how our mother grew annoyed at the noise as we excitedly repeated the circuit. Her only consolation must have been that, after burning off energy, we would sleep.

A new phase in our life was beginning. We had said goodbye to the Pratts, and I never saw any of them again. Gillian became an increasingly distant blonde memory (although one of her cousins was in my class in the primary school in Immingham). We had new neighbours, new classmates, new friends. I think, too, that the decade of the 1950s was the time when my mother felt she achieved most, as the post-war austerity gave way to slightly more affluence and opportunities – education and engaging pastimes for the boys, and for my mother the chance to pursue singing, a passionate interest since her teenage years.

But the overwhelming memory I have of my whole childhood is of a lack of *spare* cash. We were not dirt poor, as some of our neighbours and my classmates undoubtedly were – far from it; but we lacked money for frivolities and even for something like an annual holiday. My father's wages were not more than about £8 a week as a railway fireman, and rose by the time we boys left school to £16 or so, before tax, most of which he handed over directly to my mother. She was an excellent household manager, and utility bills and rent were always paid on time. But some weeks she would have just a shilling a week (5p) to spend on herself – a lipstick, perhaps, or a copy of *Woman*, or once a month *Good Housekeeping*. Our school education was free of charge – but school uniforms from the age of eleven, other clothing and footwear, hobbies, piano lessons, the Scouts and other things that make life more interesting all cost money, and there was barely enough, or so it appeared.

In order to furnish the house, Dad would frequent auction sales, coming home with a 'bargain' that was in truth nothing of the sort. For several years we sat at the dining table on bentwood chairs that had clearly been disposed of by a café, so rickety were they. Neighbours' children and our cousins were very amused; we were embarrassed. Large items were paid for on hire purchase: the first vacuum cleaner, new furniture, a radio with FM band, eventually a record player – but normally not until second-hand alternatives had been exhaustively investigated. This was long before the days of credit cards and easy money: in fact, my father never had a conventional bank account, and never wrote a cheque throughout his life. For years, Mam applied her teenage training in dressmaking to her trusty Singer treadle sewing machine and fashioned clothes for herself. She had made a jacket for me as a toddler from one of Dad's old overcoats, she tapered trousers for my brother and me, turned the collars of Dad's work shirts, and concocted costumes for fancy dress competitions at Church fêtes. My brother John once stole the show dressed as a well-cushioned fat clown; I featured as a North American redskin in a costume made from remnants; the following year I entered as a troubadour, complete with mandolin and a very itchy clip-on moustache; another time as a penguin, again deftly fashioned from remnants by our imaginative and inventive mother; and on one occasion our neighbour Ronnie Carline was dressed as a milkmaid and carried an enamel pail and a little wooden stool from our house. He was so convincing that our neighbours firmly believed he had been denied a prize because he was thought to be a girl, which, of course, scarcely counted as a fancy dress transformation.

At Barnetby primary school we took part in day trips to the seaside organised by the village Church, and in our teen years we went camping with the Scouts. But family holidays were rare. We had concessionary travel on the railways, but rarely made use of it, except to visit distant family members for an occasional weekend. In our wider family, summer holidays, for several years, consisted of being packed off to stay with an uncle and aunt in another town, to give our parents a needed break.

The first holiday I ever remember was a week out of season in a rented bungalow on the Lincolnshire coast at Humberston. Dad must have been working, because he appeared only infrequently, and my mother's sister Florrie came with her two boys for a night; another cousin also joined us for a day or two. But, perhaps in keeping with my temperament, I was not enamoured of the beach. I would play on the sand with John and our cousins for half an hour or so, catch shrimps in pools with a net, then be enticed into the water in togs run up by my mother on her Singer, only to shiver and turn blue after a few minutes (even in the sun!), then whine until I was allowed indoors to dry off. Alas, that has remained more or less the pattern throughout my life: a 'beach bum' I am not. A second holiday in Llandudno in September 1955 was a great disappointment: a street photographer captured my parents in what is obviously the aftermath of an argument. A third family holiday, in 1959, brought the family to a smallholding near Pevensey, in Sussex, for two near-disastrous weeks.

The property had been spotted in a magazine, *The Smallholder*, that my father occasionally bought, since he fancied himself as a potential poultry farmer. It seemed an ideal arrangement: we could travel that distance on a free ticket, see a part of England we had never visited, and stay in a rural setting that promised 'sea views from the estate'. My parents had rashly booked for two weeks' stay, and paid a deposit on the written assurance that there would be a reduction for the second week. The family travelled all day, crossing from Kings Cross to Victoria via Trafalgar Square and Charing Cross (in the days before the Victoria Line) and thence on the electrified Southern Region to Pevensey. We eventually found the place, about a mile up a hill from the station. Our quarters turned out to be a converted barn – actually, little more than a glorified shed, with a roof of galvanised, corrugated iron sheet – with virtually no facilities for self-catering. My mother's heart sank, but she could do nothing: a deposit had been paid and we were committed. We had to make the best of it.

After we had settled in, the farmer took us on a walk further up the hill to show us a view of the sea – some two or three miles away. That night as we lay awake, we heard what we thought was the scurrying of a mouse in our room – and the telltale droppings were visible around the cornflakes packet the following morning. A mousetrap disposed of the intruder the following night, but it was not a good omen. We made use of our concessionary travel to visit Brighton, Lewes and other places on the south coast, and mercifully the weather was good. John and I enjoyed the amusement arcades with their slot machines and jukeboxes. Johnny Kidd and the Pirates singing 'Please Don't Touch' and 'Growl' were popular hits that summer, along with Cliff Richard and the Shadows performing 'Living Doll', and I distinctly remember a beautiful curly-haired black infant of perhaps three, dressed in a blue shirt, shorts and little white socks, licking his ice-cream cone and looking up for approval as he tapped his feet in imitation of John and me as we responded to the music.

But it was clear that we were short of money. My father had lent five or ten pounds to an uncle of ours who had gone through a bad patch, and this had not been returned in time for the holiday (I suspect it never was). Family friends had lent Dad the same amount so as not to spoil the family holiday, but he refused to spend it: 'neither a borrower nor a lender be' was evidently one of his mottos. Two hours of the second Wednesday afternoon were devoted to picking blackberries for supper, and after that time in the scorching sun, my father suffered sunstroke, turned lobster-red and trembled in delirium throughout the evening. As we left for home at the end of the two weeks, the proprietor denied the promise of a reduction for the second week, made no concession to the presence of vermin, and more or less cleaned out the family's cash. Mam, who held responsibility for these matters, had forgotten to bring the contract letter with her – so she was blamed for this misfortune.

As compensation for the various disappointments, she had been looking forward to a few hours in London on the way back to Lincolnshire. But at Kings Cross, Dad noticed that there was a train going north in twenty minutes' time and insisted that we take it. My mother was disappointed, even annoyed – but Dad had the tickets, and she sat stony-faced to Retford and beyond. 'Doesn't it feel good to be on the move?,' said my father chirpily, as we headed towards Peterborough. Elsie was not amused. My parents went away together in subsequent years, but that was the last of our family holidays.

Our life in Immingham after our move from Barnetby acquired some kind of routine. After settling into our new home, we had to put in a tremendous effort to bring the garden into shape. The builders were still constructing further houses around us, and the sound of dumper-trucks, concrete-mixers, trowels, hammers and saws disturbed my father's daytime sleep, and drove our cat, Jos, crazy. After sharing our home with her for several years, during which she had lived in an outhouse, gingerly tiptoed over her first experience of snow, and given birth to a litter of kittens, she had to be put down ('put to sleep', as the euphemism had it). The garden was a mess of clay and flinty shingle, with no paths laid out, no lawns, no vegetable patches or flower beds. Dad – helped after a fashion by John and myself – put in constant off-duty hours raking rubble, breaking up old bricks to use as a foundation for concrete paths, digging, rolling a lawn area, fashioning a chicken shed and wire run, and generally exhausting himself. After several months of this tiring effort, following a year and a half of the strain of commuting at all hours between Barnetby and Immingham, and I have no doubt rumbling marital discontentment, he suffered a physical breakdown. He more or less collapsed, and was off work for several months, including a spell in a convalescent home in Kent. It was hard for John and me to understand, and I recall the shock as Dad came to chastise me for making noise in my bedroom while he was trying to sleep: he could barely raise his arm, let alone strike me. He was almost in tears.

That Christmas of 1952 must have been very hard for my parents. Dad's workmates in the ASLEF trade union rallied round and gave them a few things to put in the boys' Christmas stockings: cheap colouring books, crayons, perhaps a box of water colour paints, a few sweets; these were probably supplemented by clothing that would have had to be bought anyway. I have always appreciated the value of comradely solidarity that the union represented on occasions such as that: without the Associated Society of Locomotive Engineers and Firemen, John and I would have had a very bleak Christmas. Dad became a staunch union man, proudly wearing his membership badge and later serving as assistant branch secretary.

During his convalescence, and in subsequent years, as therapy to get his hands moving again, Dad took up knitting, including socks for John and me (with a little help from Mam to turn the heel), and he later had quite a cottage industry going with rug-making. He no longer used the snips from old pullovers and cardigans that he had refashioned in Barnetby (although those old snip rugs continued in service for many years, before ending up on the floor of a garage when the family moved to Scunthorpe), but packages of 'thrums' – long cut-off strands of wool bought by post from the carpet mills of Bradford, which Dad would wind round a wooden frame with a groove to guide a blade as he cut the threads to a length that could be knotted into canvas with a hook. For many off-duty hours during the winter, when it was too cold or wet to be working in the garden, he would sit indoors, a sheet of plastic spread on the floor to gather dust, a half-made rug on his lap and a couple of boxes of cut threads beside him, humming and singing hymns to himself as he toiled at this hobby. His obsession with this sometimes grated on my mother's nerves, but she philosophically observed that it was better he did that than spend night after night down at the pub. The rugs themselves were a product we could all enjoy, and our parents' friends appreciated them as gifts.

There were always shortages, and in the early years everything was rationed. Sweets and sugar in other forms remained rationed until well into 1953, and meat for a further year. When rationing finally ended, my mother disposed of the ration books in a ceremonial burning in our fireplace. The associated documents, the small buff National Registration Identity Cards issued after September 1939 – mine was number RLED 150, we kept as souvenirs of those grim years.

Our routine in Immingham included, from the start, a Saturday afternoon walk to a local shop, Lawson's, where John and I were allowed to choose chocolate or other sweets to the value of the coupons in the family ration books. Initially the range was restricted – and certainly nothing like the abundance of choice that is available today.

We always started with chocolate. There was Cadbury's, of course, each bar of whose Dairy Milk famously contained 'a glass and a half of full-cream milk'. I once entered a competition run by the company. I won no prize, but as a consolation – no doubt aiming to cement my loyalty to the brand – I received a little postal package containing four sixpenny bars; I'm ashamed to say that I scoffed the lot myself over the course of two days. A favourite of ours was Fry's, produced by another Quaker chocolate company, based in York (as was Rowntree's). The famous 'Five Boys', whose images appeared on the wrapper and in the advertising, introduced the rising generation to five abstract nouns, beginning with 'Desperation' and ending with 'Realisation – it's Fry's'. My mother's preference, which made an occasional entry into the household budget, was a bitter dark chocolate made by Peter's, also in York, I believe – a company that disappeared long ago, taken over, no doubt, by one of the bigger concerns.

But chocolate was not the only sugary delicacy that tickled our palates, particularly after the abolition of rationing, which allowed an abundance of flavours and shapes to tempt us. Some all-time favourites in the English repertoire of sweets are still around, including liquorice all-sorts, in sandwiches of black and white and black and yellow, or round pastels covered in pink or blue sugar balls, or cut ribbons of liquorice. And there was the coloured coconut surrounding a liquorice core – something my mother loved but Dad hated (he claimed the only foods he disliked were coconut and beetroot, but that was principally, I believe, because his diet embraced a very restricted range of flavours).

Liquorice also featured in the sherbet dip: a little pack of fizzy icing sugar, flavoured with lemon, that burst and fizzed on the tongue when licked from the liquorice dipping stick. And there was liquorice root, which appeared in the village a couple of times during my boyhood: sticks of the liquorice tree root, still with the bark intact, that we chewed to fill our mouths with the flavour of unadulterated liquorice extract. No doubt these laxative treats helped us to avoid doses of prunes or California syrup of figs.

A quite different experience was the gobstopper, which must have been every schoolboy's favourite. It was, I imagine, potentially dangerous to stuff one of these one-inch balls of hard sugar into one's mouth – imagine if we had tried to breathe in through our mouth – but it kept us quiet for an hour. Except, of course, that a feature of the real gobstopper was that each layer of sugar was coloured differently, so it had to be removed periodically from the mouth for inspection to see which part of the rainbow had been reached. A similar oral experience, but one that offered quite a different experience in taste, was the aniseed ball: hard sugar on the outside (usually coloured a deep red) but with the distinctive flavour of aniseed in the hard white centre: a preparation of our palates for *ouzo* on future Greek holidays.

We also tried pear drops, with their highly distinctive flavour that we next encountered as nail varnish remover; butterscotch, equally distinctive; and treacle toffee, just like 'ordinary' toffee, sweet and creamy, but with the dark, rich flavour of molasses. And, briefly, 'rainbow sugar puffs' – puffed wheat with a multi-coloured sugar coating.

Then there was 'kay-lai' – and I have never known how to spell it. It was essentially granulated sugar soaked in lemon essence, sickly sweet and acidic in combination, that we bought two ounces at a time, in little conical paper bags. There was only one way to consume it: lick your index finger, dip it into the bag, and suck off the sugar. It set the tongue tingling and left a satisfying yellow stain on the finger, not unlike the nicotine stain of smokers, which made us feel very grown-up.

An occasional alternative was ice-cream, but not as we know it. In those days of primitive industrial production, rather like the lumps of coal that I 'conked' to make them of usable size, in the village shop a six-inch cylinder of ice-cream would have a one-inch segment cut off and thrust into the top of a wafer cone, or a slice would be cut from a large book-sized slab and placed between two wafers. Summer trips to the seaside brought the delicacy of ice-cream cones filled by hand with a scoop, and the ice-cream van started circulating round the streets of our estate during the summer. We were allowed 'treats' irregularly, whereas some of our neighbours handed over their threepence or sixpence every day. Ice lollipops were an inferior alternative – inferior except for one shop in the village that made its own lollies using milk rather than water. Those were exquisite to my taste: fruity and creamy at the same time – and well worth paying a tanner (sixpence) rather than threepence, when the pocket money stretched so far.

All of this was far preferable to the medicinal extracts that we were also required to consume. The first was cod liver oil, usually from a spoon rather than in capsule form. Later came a thick, gloopy syrup, vaguely orange-flavoured, under the brand name of 'Robolene' or something similar, that was said to contain vitamin C, among other beneficial ingredients. It came in a large brown glass jar, and was prescribed and administered in spoonfuls as a tonic by mothers who thought their child looked 'peaky'. And a stand-by in the autumn and winter months was Owbridge's cough mixture that memory tells me contained sugar, liquorice, menthol, treacle, balsam and a variety of other ingredients to ward off the effects of damp weather. Decades later, I encountered a similar combination of flavours in a Russian vodka named *Okhotnichya*, or 'Huntsman's', drunk by Russians when out duck-shooting on cold, damp mornings. Whenever I sip it, my mind goes back to boyhood coughs and sniffles in Lincolnshire.

I settled into school as I consumed these weekly sugar rations. Immingham Church of England School – its initials I.C.E.S. were embroidered in the corner of the hand towels in the washroom – had, I think, four classrooms, each with a large coke-fuelled cast-iron stove in the corner, a wide blackboard on the wall behind the teacher's desk, and rows and rows of two-seater desks constructed from an iron frame and an ash seat and hinged worktop, with a compartment for books and writing instruments underneath and a porcelain inkwell in a hole in the corner. In my last year there, I was one of two class monitors – teacher's helpers, or (more likely) teacher's pets – whose functions included mixing the ink from powder and refilling the inkwells on a Friday afternoon from a can with a long spout. The pens had steel nibs, which rusted over time, and we were taught to write a version of the standard copperplate that Victorian scribes used in order to be legible in the days before the typewriter. The ballpoint pen had been invented by László Bíró in the 1930s, but these were still not universally available and not yet particularly cheap; in any case the ink flow was unsteady, and the pens had a tendency to leak into schoolboys' pockets. Fountain pens were the writing instrument of choice in secondary school, and they were generally no less leaky than ballpoints: the index and middle fingers of most secondary school pupils carried a tell-tale staining of royal blue or black ink. This changed as the fifties progressed – to the detriment of handwriting, including my own. The portable typewriter and the laptop were decades away.

My first teacher in I.C.E.S. was Mrs Annie Adamson, known to all and sundry as 'Fanny'. She was a no-nonsense schoolma'am of the old school, who believed in Discipline in the classroom. Through her husband Harry, a fine, deep bass singer who later gave lessons to my mother, she became a friend of my parents, but initially she inspired a mixture of fear, loathing and amusement in her young charges. A native of Halifax, in the West Riding of Yorkshire, she was a talented artist, and taught painting and drawing rather well, and she had a perfectly regular copperplate hand that was used on many occasions to adorn citations in the village, including the list of contributors to the benefit collection when the school headmaster retired. Fanny also dressed 'artistically', including wearing stockings with 'clocks' (decorative inserts of lace above the ankle), such as had gone out of fashion decades earlier.

Apart from teaching us art and the general primary curriculum of reading, writing and arithmetic, Fanny also introduced us to music. Not singing – I'm not sure she could have held a tune – and certainly not an instrument – there wasn't even a piano in her classroom – but basic musical theory, in case we should have an opportunity to engage in practical music-making. Alongside the stave, the treble clef, crotchets, quavers, minims and semibreves, we also had the rudiments of orchestral conducting. The entire class stood, facing the blackboard at the front of the classroom. To our left was a wall with windows looking out over the back playground and the playing field beyond; to the right the corridor leading to the other classrooms, the headmaster's office, the washrooms and the front playground (the toilets were across the playground at the back). Fanny instructed us in 4/4 time: raise your right hand; then DOWN – WINDOW – CORRIDOR – UP / DOWN – WINDOW – CORRIDOR – UP at the appropriate tempo. And forty-three right hands moved more or less in unison. Triple time was slightly different: DOWN – CORRIDOR – UP / DOWN – CORRIDOR – UP, and I would guess that 23 of the 43 right hands beat DOWN – WINDOW – UP (or even DOWN – WINDOW – CORRIDOR – GULP).

Fanny was a Methodist, and taught the religious instruction class to children of parents of that denomination, including John and me. She believed in thrift, which she applied to a rather unusual circumstance. Whenever any child in her class asked 'to be excused' or 'to go across the yard' – those were the permitted euphemisms – he or she was allowed to tear a single sheet of toilet paper from a roll that hung at the side of the blackboard in front of the class. On many occasions that one sheet of brittle tissue – Izal or Bronco, not the kitten-soft, puppy-strong variety that has since displaced it – would not have been sufficient, so small children must have gone home in a sad state after containing themselves until the end of class.

Also kept by the blackboard – in fact, on two nails near the top of the blackboard – was Fanny's favoured piece of classroom equipment: a three-foot, thin bamboo cane, used for the administration of her regime of ferocious discipline. Fanny must have resorted to its use twenty times a day. Its deployment came in graded steps: a kind of escalation, before that term was used to depict deterrence theory during the Cold War. Unruly behaviour could consist of all manner of disruptive activity, from chatting in class or passing a note to a neighbour to throwing paper darts or messing with the inkwell. At the first sign of such behaviour, the cane would be removed from its lodging position and placed with deliberation on the teacher's desk: this was the initial warning. If the disruptive behaviour persisted, the miscreant would be called to the front of the class and Fanny's standard punishment would be administered: a sharp strike on the fingers of the left hand. That distinguished her approach from what we read in our comics of what went on in public schools, where an exercise book thrust down the back of the trousers could, apparently, spare the delinquent pupil the full force of the punishment meted out by masters and prefects.

In Fanny's class, an unruly or noisy or chattering pupil would be brought to the front of the class, and in front of the rest of us – who were supposed to be deterred by witnessing this humiliating infliction of pain –

he (occasionally she) would be required to extend his left hand, palm up, and meekly await the blow of the cane. It certainly left a painful sting in the fingers for a few minutes. Sometimes Fanny would grasp the offender's wrist to make sure that the hand could not be withdrawn as the cane fell, but often that did not work, a child would avoid being hit, and Fanny would catch herself a blow instead. One boy from a 'rough' area of the village – ironically in the very same area where Fanny, Harry and her elder sister Agnes lived in a terraced house on Battery Street – turned this into a game of bravado, played out several times a day, every day of the week. This annoyed Fanny intensely, and her fury rose as she struggled to administer her form of justice and bring the hapless child to heel.

I suffered only once or twice, since I was altogether too timid to risk her ire, and something of a goody-goody to boot, particularly after my mother joined Harry Adamson's concert party, which brought her into regular contact with Fanny.

This was the start of a solo career as an amateur singer and singing teacher that enabled Mam to enjoy life in a way that Dad's shift work precluded. Ten or a dozen amateur singers, musicians and performers of monologues would meet in the Adamsons' house and practise round the piano, and every few weeks they would present a concert in a village hall or Methodist chapel somewhere within a thirty-mile radius. This form of entertainment, a relic of a Victorian tradition, was one of the few bright spots in a rural society that was otherwise pretty much barren of cultural existence. Arias from oratorios, music hall songs, recitals of monologues, humorous sketches, performances on the musical saw by the pianist's husband: these were the stalwarts of the repertoire, and the concert party travelled the whole of North Lincolnshire for several years. So successful were they that the local taxi firm, Sharpe's, invested in a Volkswagen minibus on the strength of their regular demand for its services.

My mother had always loved singing. As a teenager member of the Cleethorpes Ladies' Choir she had visited Blackpool, where she had a studio portrait taken. She had also, to her perpetual delight, attended a concert by the distinguished pianist Dame Myra Hess, who had graciously signed Elsie's programme. Now she had an outlet for this musical passion, and Harry offered her formal singing lessons, to train her distinctive voice. After a year or two with him, she transferred to Percy Thompson, who had organised dozens of concerts of a similar kind – in fact, over a hundred. As her singing progressed, she entered competitive musical festivals: Brigg, Scunthorpe, Cleethorpes, Mexborough, Glasgow, Blackpool, Llangollen and elsewhere, winning certificates, medals and cups and gaining valuable feedback on her technique.

Alas, her performance was not always appreciated – or, to be more accurate, she felt cheated. On one notable occasion, the adjudicator at Brigg Festival gave no explanation for his decision to award the first prize not to my mother, as her teacher and other supporters believed she deserved, but to a young tenor. My father scathingly remarked that he saw the winner put on his school cap as he left the venue, and it turned out that the young man was the son of the festival organiser, in whose home the adjudicator was staying. This, at least, was the story as we children overheard it in the adults' conversation, and it temporarily shook my mother's confidence in festivals. So did the plain fact that many of the adjudicators were not specialists in singing, so they would judge on musicality and give no useful feedback to help singers improve their technique. Still, she continued to enter them, rather than taking formal exams set by any of the musical colleges, and in later years, when she established herself as a teacher of singing, she encouraged her 'pupils', as she called them, to enter competitive festivals as a means of gaining experience and acquiring poise and confidence.

There was not much 'fun' in Fanny Adamson's class, and in 1953 I was pleased to move on to the top class at I.C.E.S. and its teacher, Miss Olive Summers, a much-loved, slightly eccentric spinster who simply adored teaching ten-year-olds. Her brother-in-law was Herbert Meakin, the headmaster, who would talk to us about his experience in the army in India and during the First World War. So affected were we by his reference to the Great War that I once shocked my father by asking him which war he had fought in, the first or the second. Mr Meakin drove to school in an ancient and somewhat temperamental Austin 7 car, which was parked outside the school gate. On chilly days, it would sometimes refuse to start, so Mr Meakin had to enlist the assistance of a pupil. More than once I was selected to sit in the driver's seat, place my right foot on the accelerator pedal, and wait while he bent over in front of the car, inserted the starter handle into a hole at the lower part of the front grille, and turned the engine with a swift flick of the wrist. My task was to listen for the engine to fire and then depress the accelerator. It usually took several attempts, and with success I would be rewarded with a lift to the bottom of my street. I felt the responsibility, but I fear that I may have flooded the carburettor on more than one occasion.

Miss Summers really engaged with the class. Not only did we progress with arithmetic, our multiplication tables, spelling, writing and reading, but we also had a range of other activities. She would sit at the piano and accompany us in patriotic songs such as 'Jerusalem', 'Rule, Britannia' and 'Land of Hope and Glory', to which we gave subversive words: 'Rule, Britannia, two tanners make a bob' and 'Land of Soap and Water', making that song an anthem to wash day. We also learned the county song 'The Lincolnshire Poacher', and songs from other counties: 'Sussex by the Sea', 'D'ye Ken John Peel?' from Cumberland (to which our elder cousins taught us ribald words), Yorkshire's 'Ilkley Moor (baht 'at)' (a perfect depiction in song of a biological food chain), Widecombe Fair (Devon), 'The Ash Grove' from Wales, and the Cornish rebel anthem 'Trelawny' ('A good sword and a trusty hand! A merry heart and true! King James's men shall understand what Cornish lads can do!').

The girls also learned to do smocking and embroidery, some more expertly than others, and were encouraged to knit. Scarves were a particular craze one year, with one stitch in four or five dropped at cast-off so that 'ladders' could be run the length of the scarf. One girl in the class decided she would knit a present for our teacher: a 'pixie hat'. Essentially, this consisted of two squares of knitted cloth stitched together on two sides so that a point appeared at the back of the head, and two ribbons stitched on the opposite corners were tied under the chin. It was not exactly a glamorous item of headwear, but Miss Summers excitedly declared that she had never had a pixie hat in her life, and she dutifully wore it to school for a few weeks. I thought it looked silly – but what did my opinion matter?

In my final term, knowing already that I had been selected to attend Barton-on-Humber Grammar School from September 1954, I was encouraged to use the school's hand loom to weave myself a scarf in my future school's colours of navy and light blue. The tension was not always perfect, as I pulled the shuttle too tightly on some rows and left it too slack on others, so that edges were a little uneven. But I had learnt how a loom works, including the technical terms 'warp' and 'weft', and I gained a sense of achievement as I wore the scarf right through my secondary school years: I still possess it, buried along with a school uniform cap at the back of a wardrobe.

We were also introduced to very basic plant biology. Once a term we would go on nature walks, identifying leaves, flowers, trees and birds. We grew broad beans in jam jars, lined with blotting paper and filled with sawdust that we watered regularly under Miss Summers's guidance – and by turning the jars we saw the effects of light and gravity on the growth of the roots and stem. We also planted orange and lemon seeds ('pips') in pots placed on the south-facing classroom window sills. There was a high rate of germination, which always provoked great excitement when a newly sown seed produced its first shoot, then leaves appeared as the seedling grew. On showery days, members of the class would be supervised as they trooped out to the playground carrying the citrus plants to stand in the rain and 'have a good drink'.

At the end of summer term, as the six-week holiday approached and the classroom equipment needed to be sorted, the inkwells washed, old steel nibs collected for disposal, and other housekeeping tasks required the attention of Miss Summers and the class monitors, we would be engaged in a competition to collect grasses, with prizes for the pupils who assembled the greatest variety, or who presented them in the most attractive way.

I generally enjoyed all the new learning experiences of my last year in I.C.E.S., which was, in retrospect, as much about inculcating the Victorian value of patriotism as giving skills and useful knowledge. Apart from the county songs, we studied from textbooks that extolled the virtues of the Empire builders, and gazed to the front of the classroom at a map that was dotted with blocks of pink: the Empire on which the sun never set. Mr Meakin's tales of his experiences in the army reinforced these values, and we gained a sense of local identity when he recounted the army slogan 'Beans and pork and Tickler's jam', since we knew of the Tickler's factory in Grimsby.

We became aware of Lincolnshire heroes and local history. Tennyson was the county's poet: born in Somersby rectory, a patriot who was made Poet Laureate by Queen Victoria, stirred up anti-Russian sentiment at the time of the Crimean War, and famously wrote 'The Charge of the Light Brigade' about one of the biggest blunders on the Anglo-French side during that war – not that we learned much of this in primary school. The brothers John and Charles Wesley, founders of the Methodist Church, came from Epworth, a village also famous for the fact that the Enclosures of the eighteenth century had not embraced the open-farmed land there. We were also made very proud of the fact that the Pilgrim Fathers sailed from Immingham creek to Holland, and thence to America, in search of religious freedom. There still stands a memorial made from stone from the original Plymouth Rock, Massachusetts, and the event was commemorated in street names in the village: Pilgrim Avenue and Mayflower Avenue.

I continued to disappoint the teachers with certain aspects of my scholarly performance. In St. Barnabas' School, Miss Freeston had commented 'Poor writing' on one of my early exercise books. In I.C.E.S., Miss Summers gave me 9 out of 10 for an English composition, and added the comment: 'English is good. Writing will look better a little smaller.' She was right, of course. I was struggling for neatness and legibility, but managing never more than five words a line. Another of my efforts was awarded 9 for content, 4 for writing, and 8 for spelling: 'Keep writing upright,' wrote Miss Summers sternly. 'Form all letters carefully.'

In a composition that I named 'The French Lesson', written at the age of ten, before I had ever taken a lesson in that language, she let the inaccurate French grammar pass. I was obviously showing off, with my explanation of the effect on pronunciation of the cedilla under the letter 'c'; but she did observe that I had written Froncaise in place of Francaise (which should in any case have had the cedilla that I had so carefully explained on the previous page), so I was required to correct that. My training in etiquette also proceeded through the English lessons: 'I was charmed with her manners' is a phrase that appears mysteriously in one of my notebooks, followed a few lines further on by 'Always raise your hat to ladies' (actually, 'laidies') – probably these were answers to a comprehension exercise.

I had little aptitude for sport, be it football in the winter or cricket in the summer, or our version of 'shinty' (which we were told was a Scottish version of hockey) that we occasionally played as a class in the rear playground. I was slightly more accomplished in the 'PT' (physical training) exercises that we performed on our little coir mats. We were not a sporting family. My father, in common with millions of other men, entered a couple of lines in Littlewood's or Vernon's football 'pools' every week, fingers crossed, hoping to win a fortune (I think he earned three shillings on one occasion). But none of us was particularly talented or skilled at any sport, and neither did we follow sport as spectators. On the other hand, I became adept at roller-skating on the pavements round our house, after receiving a Christmas present of a pair of skates; I wasn't averse to venturing on to the slides that we made in the school playground on frosty mornings; and in my later teens I enjoyed cycling and hiking in the relatively undemanding hills of the Lincolnshire Wolds: undemanding on the rise, but still exhilarating to free-wheel down the other side. But competitive games always left me cold.

I also proved a big disappointment in learning poetry. Once, the headmaster Mr Meakin came into the class and asked us each to recite a poem. Teacher's pet though I was, I was unable to recite a complete poem. All I could manage were the first few lines of Robert Browning's 'The Pied Piper of Hamelin':

> Hamelin town's in Brunswick, by famous Hanover city.
> The River Weser, deep and wide,
> Washes its walls on the southern side.

I was made to share Mr Meakin's dismay.

I did, though, learn eventually to enjoy reading ('writing' was more to my taste – putting words together in exercise books, but incapable of crafting a story or imagining a character). To the dismay of librarians and educators, along with practically all British children I was captivated by the tales of Enid Blyton. The adventures of the Famous Five and the Secret Seven stimulated my deficient imagination, and in that I was probably a typical primary school child (I was too old for Noddy and Big Ears by then). At my interview for selection to grammar school, the headmaster Norman Goddard turned to me and said, 'Don't tell me *you* like these Enid Blyton books!', to which I could only reply with the truth. As politely as possible, and with a smile, I responded: 'I do, sir!' But I had also discovered an author of far more elegantly written children's books: Arthur Ransome, whose *Coot Club* I had particularly enjoyed. Only much later did I become aware of Ransome's connections with Russia – a country and civilisation that put bread and butter, and occasionally jam, on my table throughout my adult life.

I enjoyed my couple of years in Immingham Church of England School. I quickly discovered that I was not unintelligent, a fact that was confirmed when the question arose of allowing me to try the 11-plus exam a year early. I still remembered with great fondness the blonde Gillian from Barnetby, but in Immingham there were other pretty girls whose charms generated heartache because I was too shy to take any action, even when it was expected of me by the young lady in question.

The first time that happened was at a Christmas party for the Methodist Chapel Sunday School. It must have been the year of Dad's illness, 1952, and my second Christmas in the village, and for most of the previous twelve months John and I had regularly attended the Sunday morning meeting of hymns and prayers for children that preceded the adults' morning worship. There were perhaps fifty or so children, of both sexes, at the party, held in a room at the back of the chapel. There were the usual decorations, including a tree with baubles and tinsel, and we ate sandwiches of fish paste and potted meat, tarts and cakes, and of course jelly, which I managed to consume despite my aversion to tapioca.

Then came various games, including musical chairs, pass the parcel, and a version of Postman's Knock. In the 'adult' version of the game, I later discovered, the 'postman' has no control over the identity of the recipient of the 'letter'. In a large group of nine- and ten-year-olds a different principle had to apply. On that occasion, at least, the 'postman' could actually ask for a recipient by name, and indicate whether it was to deliver a 'stamp' – which really did mean a *stamp* on the foot – or a 'letter', which meant a kiss. I was surprised, and rather perplexed, when Sandra, the prettiest girl in the village (perhaps even comparable with Gillian of blessed memory), asked for me to join her on the other side of the door, inside the dark body of the chapel, for the delivery of a *letter*! I realised immediately that something was expected of me, but I was altogether too shy to meet Sandra's expectations. There we stood in the dark for a couple of minutes. I had no sense of her feelings at that moment, and I was in a state of confusion. The door suddenly opened and we were asked whether the letter had been delivered. 'Not yet,' was the best I could manage to reply. We were given another half-minute or so, during which we may possibly have exchanged some tentative brushing of the lips. Overcome with shame, embarrassment and I don't know what other emotions, I was relieved to be allowed back to join the party, and let others who appreciated these things rather better than I did continue the game.

This experience of Sunday school was another part of my upbringing. In Barnetby, John and I had attended a Church of England school, and perhaps naturally we were sent to Sunday school in the parish church. John, indeed, was baptised in the red-brick St. Barnabas' Church as a four-year-old, since after his birth the family had been living away, and my mother's breakdown had no doubt thrown family life into disarray. I remember attending the ceremony, one Sunday afternoon, the kindly vicar the Reverend Mr Capron officiating, and Auntie Florrie and her husband Bill the principal sponsors. On one occasion, a service was held in St. Mary's Church, outside the village up a hill, and famous for its Norman lead font. That Church has long been in a state of disuse, and even in those days it could not be used in winter. I recall that at Easter we were encouraged to devote special attention to singing what Mr Capron's sister (who taught my Sunday school class) referred to as 'the vicar's favourite' hymn, 'Our blest Redeemer', the words and tune of which lodged in my memory.

In Immingham, my parents had three different Methodist churches to choose from, plus St. Andrew's Church of England. John and I were enrolled at the chapel on the corner of Pelham Road and Margaret Street, the closest to our house; our parents attended a chapel on the King's Road, at the northern end of the village. Every Sunday morning after breakfast, dressed in our 'Sunday best', including clean clothing, a white shirt, a tie, our 'best' suit, and freshly polished shoes, my brother and I were sent off for the 9.30 Sunday school service, conducted by an elderly warden and the wife of one of the stalwarts of the congregation.

The children's hymns were essentially biblical stories in song – the American spiritual about the battle of Jericho, or the parable about not cutting corners: 'The wise man built his house upon the rock ...; The foolish man built his house upon the sand... ; The rains came down and the floods came up...' with different results in the two cases (a bit like a biblical predecessor of the tale of the three little pigs). We heard stories of the life of Jesus, frequently illustrated by pictures displayed on a flannel board. We also sometimes had children's versions of the sermons that constituted a large part of the adults' service: stories with a moral purpose, or homilies on some aspect of morality. 'It's not the clothes you wear that make you a good person, the shiny shoes with the holes punched in them' (cue a surreptitious glance at one's own shiny shoes *without* holes punched in them). 'It's what you're like inside.' This was, of course, a very reassuring message to working-class kids whose parents couldn't afford to match the expensive tastes of middle-class families.

Once a year, there would be prize-giving: a special afternoon service at which children would be given prizes – usually books – for attendance. I still possess two or three of these morally sound volumes, published by the Methodist Church's own Epworth Press and therefore deemed suitable for the minds of children. For several years I was irritated to hear my name mispronounced as 'Roland' when I was called to receive my prize: that seemed even worse than my given name of 'Ronald'.

The chapel itself had, of course, an organ – hymn-singing is a strong feature in Methodism: the Wesley brothers wrote many of the songs in the Methodist Hymnal, from which my father sang as he went about his business in the garden or riding his bike home from work. But the organ in our chapel was pumped by hand, rather than by an electric motor. It was regarded as a great honour for a well-behaved older boy – never, so far as I recall, a girl – to be asked to stay behind after the Sunday school and sit beside the organ to pump for hymns during the grown-ups' service. I was occasionally invited to perform this duty, an event that evoked mixed feelings: pride at having been selected; embarrassment at having to sit facing the adult congregation for an hour or more; and sometimes disappointment that I couldn't go home and play or otherwise amuse myself.

In the same way, I discovered what went on in an adult Methodist service, including some of the rhetoric that circuit and lay preachers engaged in. In some cases, it was quite partisan: anti-Anglican and, even more, anti-Roman Catholic. But usually I was struck by the eloquence, sometimes by the passion, occasionally by the gentle earnestness as a preacher would express regret at the continuing military preparation – this was, of course, a time when the Cold War was at its height, and we were still within recent memory of the war in which our fathers and many in the congregation had fought.

It was the hymns, I think, that turned me off in the end, and the 'ordinariness' – the lack of ritual, the improvisation, as it seemed to me – of the service (combined with the lengthy sermons) and I switched to the Church of England in my teens. My younger brother had already 'defected', to my parents' disgust – a disgust mitigated by their general approval of the Reverend John Moon, the new vicar in the village: young, open, warm, who brought, so far as we as outsiders could judge, a breath of fresh air to the church. The Church of England is located on the edge of the village, and was less convenient to get to. But John, and later I, made the trek from our house on Sunday evenings for Evensong, and sometimes for Matins. John even joined the choir, and would have entered himself for confirmation, along with some of his classmates, had my parents not decreed that he was too young to decide on such a momentous matter. In my teens, I was deemed capable of deciding for myself, but the question of confirmation did not arise. I was confused by the competition between manifestations of high and low church. I could not understand some of the ritualistic bowing that some of the church wardens engaged in and others didn't, the occasional pealing of bells during a service, and other arcane details.

My perplexity was compounded when I tried to discuss some of these questions with my parents. In our circles, Roman Catholics were slightly unusual and somewhat aloof: they were excused attendance at the religious section of the morning assembly in school, and they had to go outside the village for worship. Quakers we never encountered, so I grew up thinking of them as rather exotic. Our vision was pretty limited. Dad was a Methodist, through and through, with little time for any other denomination, and an unwillingness to examine the basis of his belief. There was little value in trying to debate theology or divinity with him: all discussion – on this or any other conceivable theme – turned into an angry argument. Mam – well, her religious background was very strange. My grandfather had studied the Bible in great detail; he had abandoned institutional religion, and had gone through a fair number of the sects that stood outside the mainstream, including the Plymouth Brethren and the Jehovah's Witnesses. Rejecting them all, he reached his own interpretation of the Good Book, and became firmly convinced that he was one of the 144,000 who would be eternally saved according to the prediction of Revelation.

Given that spiritual and intellectual background, my mother was rather more tolerant than her husband, and could manifest a genuine interest in ideas, including religious ideas. She went along to the Methodist Church with my father on Sunday evenings, occasionally attended the monthly Sacrament after the evening service, and played an active part in the choir, mainly singing but occasionally conducting as well. This level of devotion continued later in life when they moved to Scunthorpe in the early 1960s. But it was hard to divine her true beliefs. To my father's disgust, she would accept copies of *The Watchtower* and *Awake!* from Jehovah's Witnesses who called at the door (and her eldest sister later joined that sect). She even allowed Mormon missionaries to come into the house and present their ideas, using flannel boards reminiscent of Methodist Sunday school to show pictures of Joseph Smith, the Angel Moroni, the prophet Lehi and the golden plates that supposedly form the basis of belief among the Latter-Day Saints.

This disagreement over religion was a further reflection, I fear, of the antipathy that developed between my parents and grew worse as the years passed. Similarly, when an old friend of the family turned to alcohol, much to my parents' distress, Mam tried to understand the condition by buying a book on alcoholism. For Dad it was simply a moral question – alcohol was, of course, forbidden to Methodists, although he did occasionally take a sip of sherry or wine or a small bottle of stout – and overcoming it was a straightforward matter of willpower.

Still, these limitations on the exchange of ideas in the home hardly impinged on my intellectual development. Within the constraints of circumstances, John and I were encouraged to get involved in whatever was going on among our peers, and above all to do well in school. Our parents were well aware of the limitations imposed by their own restricted education, and were eager for us to take advantage of the opportunities now afforded by the developing welfare state. That meant doing our best to 'pass' the 11-plus and go to a Grammar or Technical school. I remember nothing of the exam itself: it clearly was not a traumatic event for me. But there was much family satisfaction when news of the desired result came through.

Of the two grammar schools in the vicinity, I would have preferred Brigg: that was the one that a cousin of mine had attended, and the village of Barnetby was within its natural catchment area. But to attend from Immingham would have meant staying as a boarder. One or two boys managed it, but for me it was out of the question. I did not know Barton-on-Humber: we had never visited the town, apart from attending for my interview with the headmaster and another teacher, and later to buy my uniform, so it was unfamiliar, undiscovered and unexplored compared with Brigg. But being offered a place was seen as an achievement, and family and friends were all very pleased. I was both happy and sad to say farewell to Miss Summers at the end of summer term, 1954, and to friends who would not be travelling with me on the school bus to Barton.

5

B.G.S.

'Don't forget your dinner money! Have you got a hanky? Your tie isn't straight. Put your cap on!' These clipped sentences were the culmination of a frantic fifty minutes in the Hill household on my first day at secondary school. I left home, slightly agitated, at 7.50 and I'm sure my mother stood at the kitchen window in Princess Street watching me walk down the street for the school bus, my pristine new leather satchel on my shoulder, before turning her attention to getting John off to school and then settling down to her second cup of tea of the day. I shared her delight that I had been selected to attend B.G.S., even though some of my classmates would not be continuing their education with me. And on that first morning, I was as apprehensive as she must have been as she saw me off on the next stage of my life.

What I did not realise at the time was how different my life experience would be from that of friends who did not make it to the Grammar School. Even more than the knowledge and skills that I gained there, which alone would have qualified me for a responsible job, the Grammar School education opened up the possibility of education beyond: in university, first as an undergraduate, then as a graduate student and researcher, and later a career in higher education in which I never ceased to learn.

This was how my life eventually panned out, but we had no inkling in the summer of 1954 of where success in the 11-plus might take me. No one in the family, on either side, had ever been to university, and even selection for the local Grammar School, followed by what might properly be called a career, was not something that we took for granted. After selection, there was a visit to the school in the early summer of 1954 to buy my uniform from a representative of the appointed supplier, a clothing factory in Bradford. A special bus was laid on to facilitate parents, since virtually none had a car and public transport between Immingham and Barton was woefully inadequate. My parents must have been saving for months, because the cost of the uniform was a pretty sum for our family's limited means.

There was first the blazer, a two-button, single-breasted jacket in very dark navy edged with light blue ribbon. Then a cap, navy, with a band of light blue set into the fabric, a small peak, and the school crest on the front. And a tie in navy with narrow diagonal orange stripes. These were all 'official'. On top of that, we had to wear grey trousers (above the knee until we reached a certain height), a white, cream, light blue or grey shirt, grey socks, black or brown shoes, and a navy gabardine raincoat. And we also needed sports clothes: a white T-shirt (which meant owning at least two), athletic shorts – white for gym, black for football, plimsolls, football boots (in those days heavy leather, with leather studs in the sole and heel, such as have been extinct for the past forty years), and a gym bag for carrying this gear to and from school.

There were also the usual extras: a grey pullover for winter wear; a leather or canvas satchel for carrying books to and from school; a fountain pen, pencils and other items (although the school supplied all necessary textbooks, exercise books and mathematical instruments such as a ruler, a compass and a protractor, which had to be replaced if they were lost or damaged). We coped financially, at times with difficulty – yet there were some families that really struggled to support their children following their 'success' in passing the 11-plus.

Mercifully, the free school milk (one-third of a pint in little glass bottles; this was halted in the 1970s) gave us calcium and other nutrients, and the school meals service at one shilling a day ensured that my brother and I received a hot, nutritious, two-course lunch on five days a week. Meat and gravy, roast potato and cabbage or carrot; savoury mince, mashed potato and peas or swede – that kind of thing. Then perhaps Bakewell tart or jam roly-poly and custard, or sometimes a milk pudding – semolina, rice, or the dreaded tapioca – with a spoonful of jam, or rosehip syrup to add vitamin C. The hungry might have 'seconds'; those who disliked the pudding could opt for 'just custard'. Not the most exciting food, perhaps, certainly not *cordon bleu*; and since my experience in the Brumby isolation hospital in 1949 I could never swallow the tapioca even with its spoonful of rose-hip syrup. But it was at least a balanced meal that contained all we needed for health. This was a great relief to my mother, who intensely disliked cooking at the best of times: at least she could take something for granted, relax about our basic diet, and give us a very modest meal in the evening – sometimes just warm bread rolls with butter and jam or honey, accompanied by tea. The family usually had a roast at weekends, invariably garnished with the over-cooked vegetables that were my mother's staple – assisted by the pressure cooker. In comparison, the standard of cuisine produced by Mrs Wilson and her small team in the school kitchen was not at all bad.

I was certainly very excited, if a little nervous, when I headed out for the school bus on my first day in secondary school. The town of Barton-on-Humber was a good 40 minutes' journey away, and with up to a hundred pupils living in its catchment area two buses were needed to ferry sixty of them from Immingham to school each morning and home in the evening. They both set off from the village, but followed separate routes, picking up pupils in different villages on the way. The bus on which I travelled went via Habrough, South and North Killingholme and East Halton, where we picked up passengers, and thence past Thornton Abbey to Barrow and Barton. I would have to leave home not later than 7.50 to be in time for the bus at 8 o'clock, and on cold winter mornings it was quite a strain, particularly for my mother, to make sure we were up, washed, dressed, breakfasted, teeth brushed and out of the house on time. There was no time for dawdling. Catching a later bus was out of the question if we missed the official school transport: that was it for the day, apart from a solitary single-decker, green-liveried Lincolnshire Road Car public bus, sometimes driven by an uncle of mine, that went from Grimsby to Barton via Immingham and arrived at lunchtime.

Understandably, the contract for the school bus service had gone to a firm that put in a low bid, and it cut costs (and made the service viable, and presumably profitable) by using ancient vehicles of doubtful reliability. One assumes that they were safe on the road, but they were certainly old, and they were parked in the open overnight. It was not uncommon on a frosty winter's morning to be waiting at the bus stop for half an hour or more because the driver had difficulty in starting the engine, and we would arrive in Barton barely in time to reach the school for morning assembly. Occasionally it never arrived and we had an unscheduled (but not necessarily unwelcome) day off school. Very often the windows were white with the flowery patterns of frost, the ancient leather seats cold through our all-season clothing. Our breath came out as white fog for at least half of the journey.

In fact, both buses were habitually overcrowded, so that three pupils were sometimes squeezed into a double seat – an excuse, in the teenage years, for girls to sit on their boyfriends' laps on the journey to and from school. Sometimes on the homeward journey passionate kissing would delay the departure from one stop or another – near the Cross Keys Inn at South Killingholme, I particularly remember – as one of a couple had to leave his beloved until the following morning, evoking whoops, whistles and cat-calls from those of us who were anxious to get home. Nor was it unknown for hands to be slipped inside blouses, or even up skirts, as adolescents explored their emotions on the journey home.

I knew none of this when I first set out for Barton, where we were dropped off at Whitecross Street, opposite the Roman Catholic church, and followed the older pupils the quarter-mile up Caistor Road to the school. Shining new satchels (or sacks, as we called them) betrayed our status as new boys and girls just as much as our eager faces, our brand new uniforms without signs of wear or wrinkles, and our polished shoes. These same shoes would quickly become scuffed, the blazers and ties would soon earn splodges of gravy or custard, the caps would be rolled up, the peak inside the headpiece, stuffed into bulging pockets, and increasingly worn with irritation further and further back on the head.

I came to hate my cap – I managed five years with only two – and wore it with growing reluctance until after 'O' Levels, when this item of uniform was no longer required (in spite of everything, out of sentimentality I possessed both of these until the year 2012). In the 1950s, moreover, touching and slightly raising the hat was still regarded as a sign of respect, and we were required to perform this little ritual when we encountered a member of staff on the street (at least we were spared formal doffing). Indoors, of course, for a man to wear a hat was at that time considered to be the height of bad manners. How times have changed! Girls had a choice of headwear – either a navy beret with the school crest on the front, or the preferred item: a neat little 'Juliet cap' in alternating wedges of navy and light blue, again with a school crest to the front. They, of course, were not required to tip their hat when meeting teachers.

On the first morning, after Assembly, at which Mr Goddard, the head, welcomed us, we were allocated to our classes. I was in 1A, the charge of Miss Cook; 1α occupied the next classroom. The naming of the classes was, I assume, quite deliberate, since there is no hierarchy or differentiation between the Roman A and the Greek alpha. In subsequent years, however, we were distinguished according to our performance in the first-year annual exams. Using Roman numbers, those of a more academic bent were selected to take Latin in the second form, and joined IIL, while the rest were in IIM.

The excitement and curiosity as we surveyed our new classmates from numerous different primary schools was quite palpable, as was the apprehension. I was naturally shy, and the journey on the school bus had been an ordeal in itself. Introducing myself to others in the class, learning their names, trying to size them up and identify potential friends was not something that came easily to me, although I imagine Miss Cook worked hard to facilitate our socialising. I was also concerned about lunch: we had to queue for our first course, and I felt too timid to greet others at tables. Fortunately, my problem was easily resolved: we were all allocated to particular tables, each headed by a senior pupil, normally a prefect, and that was our place for the year.

I was particularly apprehensive about a vicious ritual – Americans call it hazing – that supposedly awaited newcomers, especially boys. We had heard rumours about this before we entered the place. It consisted in being seized by boys in the second form and thrown down The Valley: a nettle-covered incline at the edge of the upper sports field adjoining Caistor Road. This was bullying such as we understood went on in public schools. I think I avoided being a victim, but it certainly took place, and if perpetrators were caught they were punished by the headmaster. To my shame, I was one of the guilty bullies at the start of my second year, a time, I recall, when my behaviour deteriorated from the standards my parents and the school expected of me. This provoked critical – but not unfounded – comments from teachers in my twice-yearly report, and the occasional ticking-off from the Head. I settled down to a more disciplined life after this brief bout of delinquency.

Many pupils who lived in Barton went home for their lunch. Those of us who came from elsewhere were formally required to obtain permission to walk into town during the lunch hour. Within weeks some of my bolder classmates were heading to the sweet shops. In later years there were visits to the Singing Kettle, a café popularly known as the Stinging

Nettle, and boys would sidle to Bill's, a tobacconist who used to sell Woodbines or Park Drives in ones and twos to boys, who would smoke them in a back room in Bill's establishment or bring them to school and smoke them surreptitiously behind the cricket pavilion. I ventured in there on only one occasion, at the age of nearly sixteen, never carrying enough cash in my pocket to contemplate spending money in Barton's shops.

All this was ahead of me in 1954. I was aware that I had been one of the brighter pupils in Immingham Church of England School: after all, there had been a brief discussion about whether I should be encouraged to take my 11-plus exam a year early, as a neighbour in Immingham had done (successfully, I might add). In my case, partly because my birthday was towards the end of the academic year (but presumably mainly because my intellectual development was not up to the required standard), it was decided not to put my candidature forward. I must have been reasonably intelligent, but it took me quite some time to place myself in comparison with my fellows.

After the initial excitement combined with bewilderment, my class-mates and I found our way round the school, we settled down and began to have our minds expanded by teachers who confronted us with materials that were quite new to our experience. The routine was very different from primary school, and took some getting used to: the notion of moving to different classrooms for lessons in various subjects, for example, or having specialist teachers for disciplines, and having a programme of set homework of so many subjects each evening, each expected to take 15–30 minutes. In the first week, we were each given a hymn book, for use at the daily morning assembly, and by tradition used as an autograph album in our final week in the school. If lost, it had to be replaced at our own (or our parents') expense.

We were supplied with textbooks for our courses, and encouraged to take them home and cover them in stout brown paper to preserve them; they remained school property, so we were not supposed to write in them. We received a set of exercise books with the school crest boldly printed on the front cover, one for each subject, and colour-coded: orange for biology, green for English, blue for French, and so on. And we were also given a much thicker 'general exercise book' for taking rough notes or doing work in class, which was reproduced in a fuller, neater version in the subject notebooks. This was expected to suffice until mid-year, when a second general exercise book was supplied. With experience, and increased dexterity with the pen, the handwriting in the preliminary versions of our class notes grew smaller and smaller in order to ensure the available space lasted the course. Half-size notebooks were used for vocabulary, say, or grammatical explanations or other reminders to ourselves.

From the start, and with increasing severity, I found that no one in my family could help me with homework: both parents had left school at the earliest permissible age – fourteen – in 1933, and their formal education had ceased. In subsequent years, my mother did help me with French vocabulary. She knew not a word of the language herself, but when I gave her my little vocabulary notebook, with English words on the left of the page and French on the right, she would combine assistance with a humdrum task such as ironing, asking me a word, to which I would give the French, if I knew it. She could just about work out whether the word I pronounced sounded similar to the letters in front of her, and I could explain where a French combination of letters stood for a different sound from their pronunciation in English. It worked pretty well.

That was several years ahead. In the first week of term in September 1954, I had no idea of what to expect when Mr Brice came in and introduced us to the language. He was tall, bespectacled, with a long face and a kindly demeanour, wavy hair combed straight back from the forehead, and somewhat bushy eyebrows. After distributing a copy of the textbook to each pupil, he read the opening paragraph, in order to give us a notion of the sounds of French. The phrase 'la rue Royale', containing two sounds that do not exist in English, was designed to demonstrate the challenges of spoken French. To make us feel more comfortable about making unfamiliar sounds, the book pointed out that the average Frenchman or woman would have great difficulty in saying 'the twelfth month'. Neither the textbook nor Mr Brice reminded us that an Irish child, or a Cockney, would likewise have difficulty with that particular English phrase. In North Lincolnshire we could manage it reasonably well – although the 'o' in *month* would have sounded odd to southerners.

Over the next couple of weeks, we were introduced to the phonetic alphabet, and given a vowel chart to indicate the parts of the mouth in which various sounds are formed. It all made a lot of sense to me, although I recall that most of my classmates found it incomprehensible, despite Mr Brice's efforts. I managed to acquire what seemed to be a passable accent in French, although when I later did a course in French phonetics at Leeds University I had to take measures to correct my pronunciation of the French 'o'.

Before long, as the first-formers became acculturated to the norms of the school, we discovered that Mr Brice was referred to as 'Billo' by pupils of all ages; his colleagues on the staff knew him as 'Wilfie'. He was formally the Second Master, and had been in the school since its opening in 1931. His principal subject was French, but he had also taught Latin, and even basic science, in the school's early history. Apart from his teaching, he was responsible for the onerous business of devising the timetable for a school of about 350 pupils, divided into two streams: 1A and 1α, which was of no significance regarding curriculum, followed by IIL – which focused on the more academic disciplines – and IIM and so on up to Form V, the 'O' level year, and then a Lower and an Upper Sixth Form, divided into Arts and Science.

As the school expanded to embrace Baysgarth House, located a few hundred yards down the road, he had to timetable walks from the main campus to the annexe for teaching staff, entire classes, or both. It was a pretty thankless task, and I imagine, looking back, that he was not appreciated. Certainly, when the original Senior Mistress and Deputy Head Miss Nightingale (known as 'The Bird') retired in 1956, Billo was not made Deputy Head, even though in practice he had been performing functions normally allocated to someone of that status. He must have felt irritated, or at least disappointed, when Miss Carr, young, unmarried and somewhat attractive (well, my Dad fancied her!), replaced 'The Bird' as Senior Mistress and performed the public functions of Deputy Head, including officiating at Speech Days, the formal celebratory occasions in the autumn term on which prizes were distributed. But he carried on stoically, and if he felt sensitive to these matters none of that showed to us pupils. He would come in and cheerfully do his teaching, frowning quizzically when he noticed that someone (I fear I was the guilty one) had changed his spelling of Flaubert on a blackboard to 'Phlaubert', and occasionally muttering to himself something to the effect that 'standards are falling'. He had a tiny office beside the entrance to Baysgarth House, where we would see his trusty Raleigh bicycle, with its greying saddle-bag sometimes bulging with our exercise books, parked outside come rain, come shine.

SCHOOL ENTRANCE TO BAYSGARTH HOUSE, AND THE PARK BEYOND.
'BILLO'S' OFFICE WAS TO THE RIGHT OF THE DOOR

It was Billo who inspired an interest in languages, and in learning how to pronounce them accurately, that has stayed with me. Phonetics doesn't work for everyone, but it certainly taught me how to analyse a sound, to work out which parts of the mouth are used to utter it, and then to work on that sound in combination with others to achieve a reasonable approximation to a native speaker. As I learned other languages, either as part of my formal study at Leeds University (where I read Russian) or as a hobby (picking up German, Polish, some Dutch, a smattering of Romanian), I have always remembered Billo as I applied the ears that he trained and the theory that he imbued to the task of sounding as near a native as I can manage. Some do it by ear; I do it on the Billo principles. And, thanks to Billo, I have been complimented on my pronunciation of the several languages with which I am familiar.

A part of the same lesson was that individual letters and combinations of letters are pronounced very differently in different languages; or, to put the same thing the other way round, individual sounds are rendered differently in the various languages of Europe, to the extent that one needs to know which language one is dealing with before knowing how to pronounce the words. The letter 'j' sounds quite different when pronounced in English, French, German or Spanish; the letter 's' and the combination 'sz' are pronounced in opposite ways in Hungarian and Polish; the combination 'ch' likewise represents several different sounds – even in English. And this is before one gets to the intricacies of diacritics (accents), which distinguish Continental languages at least as much as orthography. Thanks to Billo's punctilious instruction in these basic matters, I acquired a sensitivity that perhaps most English readers of the Latin script never pick up (they don't need to, after all), and it was invaluable in my later career as a scholar and editor.

This has both drawbacks and advantages. In a European country I can at least pronounce the names of streets, but by the same token, I wince when I hear public representatives or broadcast journalists wildly mispronounce the names of visiting foreign dignitaries or the names of places from which they are reporting. Sheer professionalism would impel me to make inquiries, although the newsreader Angela Rippon was lampooned for giving foreign terms an authentic sound. I have always found these questions fascinating, and I attribute this fascination to the inspiring example of Billo and 'la rue Royale'.

In later years, and with other teachers, we played charades in French, recited poems, and learned French songs, including a reprise in French of 'Little Arabella Miller' from Miss Freeston's class in Barnetby:

> Quand trois poules vont au champ
> La première va devant.
> La seconde suit la première,
> La troisième est la dernière.
> Quand trois poules ...

'When three hens go to the field, the first goes in front, the second follows the first, and the third one is last.' Pretty logical, as Billo noted.

Another that sticks in the mind is the well-known French-Canadian 'L'Alouette', an equivalent of the American Negro spiritual, 'Dem bones', in which the head bone's connected to the neck bone, the neck bone's connected to the shoulder bone, and so on, down to the toe bone connected to the foot bone. Learning to pluck the feathers from different parts of a bird is not a bad way of teaching children the vocabulary of the body. And there was 'Jeanneton', with a few 'alouettes' thrown in as fa-la-la folksong lines, in which a country girl, on her way with her sickle to cut rushes, meets three handsome lads. The first, 'un peu timide', greets her very politely; the second, a little less well-behaved, strokes her chin; and the third, 'un intrepide', tries to kiss her. All very enlightening for adolescent children in a mixed-sex school – a prelude for the 'sex education' that later came in the biology class.

In the 1950s, we took it for granted that both our primary and our secondary schools were co-educational. There were separate entrances for boys and girls, and by and large there was division – not quite segregation – in the classrooms, with boys on one side and girls on the other. Games were played separately, of course, and there was some distinction in the curriculum: girls did not do technical drawing or woodwork, and it was only very rarely that a boy took domestic science, which largely meant sewing and later cookery (although in one year a boy won the prize for that subject). But as we advanced through puberty into adolescence and approached adulthood, we could not fail to be aware of the opposite sex, even in a society that was far less obsessed with sex than today. There was significant overcrowding in the school, and not enough space in the cloakrooms, so sometimes girls changing after sports would be obliged to use the corridor. It must have been very embarrassing for the girls as hormone-charged teenage boys walked by, sometimes declining to avert their eyes as they caught glimpses of underskirts, thighs and the occasional suspender belt. The 'liberty bodices' of primary school – front-buttoned, tunic-like undergarments – had given way to altogether more enticing garb.

Inevitably liaisons happened, in a shifting web of romantic associations, hand-holding, surreptitious kissing, occasional groping. One of the tasks of the prefects was to flush out any such activity behind the cricket pavilion. Anything more serious, entailing the excitement of skin on skin and the pleasures of intertwined limbs, was mainly confined to hours out of school. There were occasional pregnancies, about which parents tut-tutted without seriously discussing the matter with their own children. I say that as a son of parents whose emotional and sexual life was, in their own confession, less than relaxed or passionate: perhaps daughters had more understanding relationships with their parents.

Languages were by far my best subjects throughout my years at B.G.S., although I enjoyed mathematics and was reasonably good at physics and chemistry. History was interesting, particularly the account of the development of democracy in nineteenth-century Britain; geography widened my horizons, although I had to give that up after the third form, at the age of fourteen; even technical drawing and woodwork attached me mentally to my grandfather, from whom I may have inherited some manual skill.

After Billo, the second teacher who had a profound influence on me was Henry Treece, well known as a poet and novelist, particularly his historical novels for children, but also a sometime boxer, among other distinctions. In my first year at B.G.S. he took our class for English and Art. Apart from the two children's novels that we read in class – Thomas C. Hinkle's *Shag, The Story of a Dog* in the first half of the year and, after exchanging books with the pupils in 1α, *Bran, the Bronze-smith* by Joyce Reason – Henry introduced us to sentence structure. We learned the basic terminology that enabled us to distinguish sentences from phrases and clauses, and we applied to English some of the grammatical categories that we were also learning in French. He explained what a pun was ('He had a hole in his trousers, but it was notwithstanding'), and a metaphor: 'Gather ye rosebuds while ye may,' he said whimsically to an 'O' level class in the spring of 1959, adding with a grin, 'but don't let me catch you gathering rosebuds.' In subsequent years Latin gave a firmer grounding in the ideas of grammar and syntax, but I certainly came away from that first year's English course with an idea of what a sentence is – something that now appears not to have been taught in schools for many years. As I acknowledged in the preface to one of the academic textbooks that I wrote many years later (and dedicated, with deep respect and gratitude, to the memory of Henry Treece), 'if my prose possesses any clarity or elegance, then much is due to his early guidance; and his lively and broad-ranging teaching style taught me that there is more to training a mind than bowing to the demands of an examination curriculum.'

I was, I suppose, romantically intrigued by the idea of being a writer of books. From a young age, I had wanted to own a typewriter, and I later aspired to a printing press. As a small boy I received as a Christmas present a 'John Bull Printing Outfit', and I loved using the tweezers to place the rubber letters in reverse into the grooves of the wooden block, then taking ink from a pad and making an impression on paper. It was all very satisfying, a fact that may have been a reflection of my poor handwriting, as Miss Freeston had pointed out in my first year at St. Barnabas' school.

But the eagerness to be published was something that I caught from Mr Treece. I was not the only pupil of his who was impressed. The Sixth-Form Library had a book written by Marjorie Boulton, daughter of the first headmaster, which she had dedicated to Henry Treece, 'the best teacher I have known'. In the third form, he entertained us to some of the more esoteric aspects of English composition, including the order in which punctuation marks appear – the *Chicago Manual of Style* or the *Oxford Dictionary for Writers and Editors* or *Hart's Rules for Printers* long before I was ever aware of these editorial *vademecums*. Along with the study of other languages with different conventions or rules, I found this approach to reading and writing English quite engaging, even fascinating, and it was of great value when I started writing myself, and decades later took on editorial functions for academic journals and publishers. Sentence structure, word order, grammatical 'agreement', punctuation selected to indicate which words relate to others in a sentence: these, I realised, are far more important than spelling in presenting one's ideas clearly. And a course to prepare for an exam called 'Use of English' in the Sixth Form gave further practice and taught that there are different registers in a language, and that the language of a weekly comic is not appropriate in a job application or when writing to one's MP. These long-established conventions are even more apposite in the age of the txt msg and tweet.

If the initial training in writing that I received from Henry Treece's classes was of permanent benefit, I'm afraid he was less successful in teaching me literature – and the same goes for his colleagues. Unlike many in the school, I confess, I was never a great reader. I also suffered in the same way that millions of other working-class children from around the world have done (including, the Soviet Union, as my professional training subsequently taught me): through the lack of appropriate cultural supports in the home. Our house had few works of literature in it, and my parents never read for pleasure. The daily paper, originally the *News Chronicle* and later the *Daily Mail*, a weekly women's magazine when the budget stretched to it, and in my father's case The Bible (Dad always wrote 'shew' rather than 'show'): this was more or less the extent of the reading matter that engaged the attention of the adults in the household. Fiction was something that my father simply never bothered with, and my mother explicitly rejected it, despite her keen participation in amateur dramatics, preferring books and stories with a factual basis. Years later, for a decade or more, monthly issues of the *Reader's Digest* arrived by post, and later volume after volume of condensed books from the same source. There was little evidence, though, that these collections were ever read – and the same goes for the monthly magazine. As a reader, I plodded – still do, to some extent – so that getting through a 250-page novel was a major task; *Great Expectations*, *Vanity Fair*, *Germinal* or

War and Peace posed a challenge, requiring the commitment of a substantial block of time. And reading a few pages in bed before turning off the light would mean that I would actually lose the plot as the reading of a single novel extended over several weeks.

In B.G.S. I could probably never read faster than about twenty pages an hour, and I never acquired the skill of rapid reading. This has been a handicap in my subsequent career, and I have sometimes wondered whether the more practical life of a scientist might have suited me better. But there was more to it than that. None of my teachers of English, French, or later Russian literature could ever explain what the point of 'studying' literature was. When with Henry Treece we studied Shakespeare's *Julius Caesar*, he brought alive in my mind the *craft* of the playwright in setting up the actors on the stage to murder Caesar. When, in A-level French literature, we engaged in exercises known as 'explication de texte', I could examine the images, the figures of speech, the assonance and alliteration, the allusions, and make sense of it. Such an exercise again revealed the craft of the writer. I could also apply similar techniques to English: seeing the point of meandering sentences in this passage and staccato phrases in that. All this revealed something of the writer's skill in evoking a mood, identifying a character or telling a gripping tale.

But that was not what the study of literature seemed to be about. We were supposed – or so it seemed – to 'get something' out of the works that we were studying, but what that something was eluded me. We studied the poetry of Wordsworth – 'Michael', 'The Leech Gatherer' or 'Daffodils' – and Keats – 'The Eve of St. Agnes', 'To Autumn', 'Izabella, or the Pot of Basil' – and I memorised select passages to illustrate certain features. But the questions that we were required to answer seemed not to relate to what we had read, but to other matters. We were told that Wordsworth strove to make his verse *accessible* to everyone, and we could find suitably trite passages to illustrate the point, most famously

> I've measured it from side to side:
> 'Tis three feet long, and two feet wide.

But we were not allowed to say that he failed in his goal when he wrote of 'intimations of immortality' or gave a poem the title 'Expostulation and Reply'. The *accessible* version (even though it means something slightly different) is 'Question and Answer', so why the highfalutin' language? Was the poet just showing off? Or was he a phoney?

To help make sense of literature – or at least to be able to produce plausible, if not convincing, essays and exam answers – I compiled pages and pages of quotations: from Chaucer, Shakespeare, Byron, Wordsworth, Keats and all the other poets and novelists whose work we were studying. Yet, asked to 'Show how the Pardoner's Tale blends melodrama and a strict moral code', my six and a half pages of sweated-over prose elicited the comment: 'All this has very little relevance to the title; you have the material but you have not used it – in spite of the fact that I told you how to set about it.' This devastating critique was accompanied by a grade of 'D', followed by the stern instruction: 'Repeat'. I duly repeated, and was awarded a 'B(+)', but I remained uncertain about the *purpose* of this and other exercises. How did you know that you'd got it right?

My experience was perhaps that of many millions for whom literature as a school subject for examination was turned into a task, a chore, rather than a source of pleasure and enjoyment – and it is only in my retirement that I have taken to regularly reading classic or even modern literature for pleasure.

One specific lesson I do recall from Henry Treece's 'O' level course. The prescribed anthology of poetry included the American folksong 'Bluetail Fly', in which American performers invariably sing the chorus as 'Jimmy Crackcorn'; some even give that name to the song, and I wonder if they ever think about what the words might mean. The poet in Henry Treece understood what the song is about: a kind of lament by a slave whose (unusual) *kind* master has been killed in a riding accident; the grieving slave – perhaps fearing a future under a cruel new owner – begs for the simplest food, if only that could bring back his master:

> Gimme cracked corn and I don't care:
> My master's gone away.

We were impressed to discover that Henry's 'War Poem' was in the same collection, although it excluded the poem that is most frequently associated with his name, 'Lincolnshire Bomber Station', in which the poet reminds his reader that the bitter, damp cold of Lincolnshire in the Second World War was precisely the cold that the Romans had endured as Legions of the Eagle – the title of one of his best-known children's novels.

The most important educational lesson that Henry Treece taught me, however, was that education is not about passing exams and sticking rigidly to a prescribed syllabus. He had a wide range of knowledge and interests, which he inculcated into us pupils. An 'English' lesson could turn into a disquisition on Greek architecture: from his lips I learned the differences between Doric, Ionic and Corinthian columns; or an exposition of some of the rules of heraldry, including the terminology: quarters and chevrons, lion *passant, rampant* and *guardant*; *bend sinister*; *gules, azure, argent* and *or*. This was necessary background for reading Keats's 'Eve of St. Agnes', since through the 'casement, high and triple-arched' the moon 'threw warm gules on Madeleine's fair breast', and rose hue on her hands and amethyst on her cross, even though it was pointed out in class that moonlight does not cast colour through stained glass: this was an example of 'poetic licence'.

Henry was a talented artist, too. Under his guidance we tried painting, drawing in pencil, ink, pastel and charcoal, and lino-cutting, which was new to me. I almost stabbed myself with the cutter, and my picture was of no merit whatsoever, but I learned a bit of technique. I also picked up a method of handling rowdy students. Sometimes, when Henry was in the back room mixing paint or whatever, we pupils would start chatting, then talking noisily, almost shouting – all teachers are aware of this when their back is turned. After three or four minutes, Henry would emerge into the classroom, bellow 'SHUT UP!', and to the class of twelve-year-olds, now in shocked silence, he would give a broad smile, turning into a grin. The technique still worked when on a Monday morning four decades later I would confront a class of 400 undergraduates some of whom were more interested in discussing their weekend than in listening to my lecture.

Henry remains something of a hero, and I remember so many details that inspired me. He grew a moustache at one point, and weighed himself on the school scales during his weekly lunch supervision: was he joking, or was he taking himself a little too seriously? For a period of several weeks or months, he would come to school wearing a navy beret and a scarf – perhaps he was going through a Francophile phase. He drove a Sunbeam Alpine sports car, and we heard that one of his favourite pursuits was driving it in the Spanish mountains. He was in touch with young people and their tastes: he once suggested that we might celebrate some success or other by wearing 'the fadedest blue jeans you could imagine'. When new honours boards were made for the school – by the woodwork master, Mr Millet – the B.G.S. crest above each was painted by

Henry Treece (but, curiously, what was a white background in the lower half of the escutcheon he painted dark blue). His real interest was writing, and not just for children, but he kept the 'day job' as long as his health permitted, fearing a printers' strike or a paper shortage – or perhaps afraid that fluctuating royalties might not always pay the bills. We missed him when he suffered a heart attack and was out of school for some time, and his death in 1966, a few years after I left the school, was something that truly moved me. Those who were in his class in particular years learned from him the art of story-writing – something I never mastered. Might he have discovered a spark of talent in me that could have been developed? I shall never know. Life followed a more prosaic course.

I remember other teachers, of course. One was 'Bim Bom', as we called the biology master, Mr Benn, who arrived at the start of my second year. Short, slightly stooped, wearing tortoiseshell glasses and what I think of as a squadron-leader's moustache, he appeared lazy, slumped in his chair on a raised dais behind the bench at the front of the classroom. On successive school photos he seemed to be sleeping. But he had the right sense of humour to deal with adolescent teenagers.

The amoeba and spirogyra we had covered under his predecessor Mr Smithson, in the biology classroom, with its formaldehyde-preserved specimens and its board-mounted half-skeleton of an elderly female, known affectionately as 'Granny' (we assumed that Granny's literal other half was in another school). With 'Bim Bom' we learned about osmosis and photosynthesis, the bones of the skeleton, the functioning of the liver and kidney, the circulatory system and – most importantly for teenagers – reproduction. As the textbook pages on that eternally fascinating topic came closer lesson by lesson, giggles disrupted each class for a couple of weeks beforehand. Eventually, in exasperation 'Bim Bom' directed his stern gaze at one fourteen-year-old girl: 'Calm down, Miss Dent', he said – a sign of seriousness, since girls were normally addressed by their Christian name, boys by their surname, none by a title. 'We shall be coming to reproduction next!' And so we did, in the rabbit, of course. It was only in a sixth-form course in Human Biology that some of us studied 'the facts of life' in humans (along with how to brush one's teeth, and how a domestic hot water system works).

We were amused by what seemed to be Bim Bom's idiosyncrasies. One pupil, Marie Swanson, he always addressed as 'Gloria', after the film star. He would dictate our class notes verbatim, including punctuation. 'The blood consists of – *two dots and a dash* – *new line* – *one inch from the margin* – 1 – *bracket* – *capital P* – Plasma – *open bracket* – 55% in man – *close bracket* – *new line* – *one inch from the margin* – 2 – *bracket* – *capital C* – Corpuscles – *open bracket* – 45% in man – *close bracket* – *new line* ...'. We would follow these instructions in our exercise books, with greater or lesser fidelity:

The blood consists of :–
1) Plasma (55% in man)
2) Corpuscles (45% in man) ...

When demonstrating an iodine test to show the presence of starch in bread, he took out a slice of *brown* bread for the purpose – unusual in North Lincs at that time. We giggled. 'Yes,' said Bim Bom, 'we eat brown bread in our house; we can't afford white.' When chattering broke out as he turned to write something on the blackboard, he immediately identified the culprit, informing the class that 'When they qualify, all teachers are given eyes in the back of their head.' And if he heard coarse language being used, he reminded us that he was quite familiar with such vocabulary: 'Don't forget, I've been to university.' He told the story of the young Yorkshire lad taken to the Methodist chapel one Sunday morning by his mother; as he rose for the final hymn after a long sermon, his soprano voice uttered the memorable line: 'Ee Mum, by gum, my bum is numb!' Bim Bom also used an interesting code to identify a set of textbooks that our class shared with another group. 'Turn to page 99,' he said, conspiratorially. We dutifully did so. 'Now, take your pen, and put a dot inside the second figure nine.' Those books were now associated with Bim Bom's class.

He was one of the teachers some of us enjoyed mocking, in a friendly way, of course. On one occasion, when writing up his homework on the digestive system, a classmate, David Jones, deliberately referred to 'waist products', and explained it by saying he had been watching the Miss World competition at the time. And when he introduced us to the *glomerulus* – a knot of capillaries inside the kidney that helps filter the blood – Bim Bom's Yorkshire pronunciation, with a slight trill of the 'r' in the middle of the word, set us off hilariously imitating him.

Mr Benn was also a keen amateur musician, and since there was no professional music teacher in the school he took classes in which he introduced us to the broad history of classical music from Bach and Handel through Haydn, Mozart and Beethoven, Schubert and Mendelssohn at least as far as Liszt. He also directed the school choir. On one occasion, finding himself short of a tenor voice or two, he approached me, aware that I did a bit of singing, and asked what top note I could reach. 'About G, sir,' I said. 'Well, if you stood on a stool, do you think you could reach an upper C?' During my third year – the last in which I did woodwork – Mr Benn would come in during a two-hour class and engage in a labour of love, under the direction of the genial Mr Millett: the creation of an attractive double piano stool, with shapely Queen Anne legs, all French polished with a seat upholstered in velvet. We boys, meanwhile, sawed away at our tenons, chiselled our mortises, planed our rough timber with a hand plane (complete with 'five-eighths Whitworth cheesehead set-screw') or fitted the rails to the stiles of our sample door for a cupboard that might one day adorn our bedroom walls. When I arrived in Leeds University after leaving B.G.S., I discovered that one of my more eccentric lecturers in French was a Dr Benn, an uncle of my former biology teacher.

Chad – William Neville Chadwick – also arrived in our second year in B.G.S. to teach mainly Latin, and also some sport and gymnastics. A Yorkshireman, educated at Cambridge University after military service, he appreciated early on that I was not adept at team sports, so he enjoyed putting lots of spin on a cricket ball so that I could not possibly get my bat to make contact as it bounced in a completely unpredictable direction. I was quite hopeless at that quintessentially English game, and at soccer, the winter sport available to boys (girls had hockey in the winter, tennis and rounders in the summer). I couldn't kick straight, or 'trap' the ball as it landed near my foot; and as for heading it – no way! Occasionally towards the end of term, Chad let his Yorkshire roots emerge and he encouraged a game with 'the right-shaped ball' – oval, not spherical. I learned a little about scrums, lineouts and downward pressure on the ball to score a try, followed by a conversion, but I proved no more skilful at Rugby than at soccer or cricket. Or at tennis, come to that. One summer when I was about fifteen, I acquired a cheap tennis racquet and spent hours in a tennis club at Habrough, making little progress with my serve, backhand or volley. When the clubhouse was taken over (mainly by others) for romantic encounters, tennis took a back seat.

I have often wondered whether my lack of sporting ability or even interest in team games arose from my temperament as a loner, or perhaps from my lack of a competitive spirit, or from unfortunate experiences such as being struck on the nose by a cricket bat in Barnetby primary school, or simply from an inability to get my limbs to do what was required of them. Chad observed that I had a neat technique on the vaulting-horse, and he encouraged me in gymnastics, but the opportunities didn't exist to take it very far. With my long legs, I could also run reasonably well, and some field events were just about within my competence. But I was no match for my really athletic classmates, and there was little encouragement for those who came outside the first half-dozen in whatever sport. Being perpetually fourth in a race is of little use – except in a relay, where I was once part of a record-breaking junior team for Gaunt House.

A result is that as an adult I have no interest in sport, as either participant or spectator. Football, cricket, tennis, baseball, golf – I have never been able to raise enthusiasm for what strike me as the *antics* of 'professionals' for whom winning at whatever cost (even deliberately cheating – that is, disregarding the very spirit of sportsmanship), for exceptionally high rewards, turns them into a branch of show business rather than sport. The enthusiasm of Olympics participants does sometimes infect me; but the intrusion of various forms of cheating in recent decades destroys the point, as far as I am concerned. Unlike my classmates, who turned out on Saturdays week after week to play for the school against other schools in the region, I had neither the talent nor the interest – and that lack has stayed with me throughout my life. With certain pursuits, such as reading or music and my limited appreciation of the Arts in general, and even my restricted understanding of science, I feel it is my loss. I earnestly wish I could be Renaissance Man. My lack of interest in sport gives me no such sense of deprivation. When I unadvisedly attended a college football game in America, after ten minutes' bafflement I found concentrating on the cheer-leaders a far more attractive proposition.

Even in running, I lacked the stamina to become a real performer. I could sprint the one hundred yards, and sometimes come in the first three – but rarely could I win. Longer distances were beyond me, and in the annual cross-country I would come in somewhere in the mid-field. To my shame and slight regret, at the age of fifteen, along with others in the class, I treated the race as a joke, starting off at little more than a walking pace. I couldn't keep up the pretence, though, and I did make a move, picked up my pace, left my laggard friends behind, pounded strongly past several dozen weaker runners and came in at a semi-respectable thirty-fifth or so.

The final joke was in the Upper Sixth, when by tradition a staff team took on the senior girls at hockey. As the school's Head Boy, I was asked to fill in a gap on the staff team, not because I was perceived to have talent, but presumably because I was no more (or no less) fit or talented than some of the staff who were more than twice my age. From contact with girls on the team, I knew what 'bullying off' meant, and had a vague understanding of the 'turning' rule, but since I had never so much as picked up a hockey stick in my life (shinty, at Immingham primary school, was the closest I had come), my skills, if any, were at best untested. I later confessed in the school magazine, *The Bartonian*, that I had 'gained a great deal of enjoyment' from the encounter, even though 'I seemed to spend more time lying on the ground than standing on my feet.' The staff won, by a score of three goals to nil, but that concluded my career as a hockey player, or as an active participant in any team sport.

As a university student, I tried judo for two years running, hoping that I might manage an individual rather than team sport. I bought a *judogi* (the thick, pyjama-like, white judo suit) and dyed red tips on my belt – red being the colour of the novice, which I expected to be allowed to snip off within a few weeks on becoming a white belt, the lowest grade. I learned how to avoid serious injury when falling, engaged in *randori* (free practice) and practised my *hanai-goshi*, *harai-goshi* and *o-goshi* throws for several weeks on each occasion. But after pulling a thigh muscle and falling on my head too many times in the first few bouts with experienced *judokas*, I decided that this sport was not for me, any more than a team game was. I retired hurt, and the *judogi* languished unworn in the back of my wardrobe until I eventually decided to throw it out. I was not, I concluded, cut out for sport, apart from a bit of running, in mid-life, and walking – none of it competitively. I am emphatically *not* to be confused with the very distinguished marathon runner, Ron Hill, whose career achievements more than compensate for the sporting weakness of the namesake he has never met.

In Latin, though, as in French, I was more talented, and Chad encouraged me, set me additional exercises, and coached me for 'S' Level (a national exam that was superior to 'A' Level). I failed in that, again (I think) because the study of literature let me down. How I managed an 'S' level in French, which also contained much literature, I shall never know –

MYSELF AND FRIENDS IN UNCHARACTERISTIC MODE

but I do remember snippets of Hugo, Mallarmé and Verlaine, and of Molière and Maupassant. I was one of only two pupils who took 'A' level Latin, the other being Rhieta Lewis, and I suppose we were supportive rivals. She had a far greater affinity with literature than I had, and indeed later taught French and Latin in a secondary school. Upper Sixth Form included the occasional 'field trip' with Chad, visiting excavations of a Roman villa at Winterton and museums in Scunthorpe and Lincoln to look at Roman remains and read up some of the Roman history of the region – the very history that Henry Treece brought to life in his children's novels.

Chad was the only teacher, along with his wife Edith (we first knew her as Miss Salt), with whom I retained regular contact after leaving the school. We exchanged Christmas cards and letters, and I occasionally visited him, until his death in 2011. I had much sympathy and affection for him: his subject was becoming deeply unfashionable, an arthritic hip prevented him from continuing with sport, and when the school was forcibly merged with the Beretun School under the policy of comprehensive secondary education, he felt there was little real future for him. He once mentioned that he regarded himself as potentially headmaster material – but he would not want the hassle. He abandoned his ambition, retired very early, developed a magnificent garden (and, of course, knew the Latin names of all the trees and shrubs), and with Edith enjoyed travelling with their caravan, particularly to watch Rudolf Nureyev dance, in Britain and on the Continent.

I remember, too, Jack Baker, John ('Horace') Hopley, Denis ('Leggy') Lawson, Freddie Manning, and Ken Shipstone – a handsome Leeds graduate who came in 1959 to teach history, had the sixth-form girls swooning, and joined a group of us sixth-formers during lunch break with his sonorous acoustic guitar. Not all taught me, although some tried to do so. One Wednesday afternoon when the fifth form were being supervised at cricket by Jack Baker (employed principally as a geography teacher), I was half-heartedly pretending to bat, not having bothered to change my shirt. Jack told me to buck up my ideas and get my collar and tie off. So I did – I removed both my tie *and* my separate collar, upsetting Mr Baker, who said that was not what he called a cricket shirt. He was right, of course.

'Leggy' Lawson likewise had little success in improving my skills with the cricket bat or football. Young, rather suave, with a perfect Windsor knot in his tie, the regular accompanist on the piano at the morning assembly, he cut a rather dashing figure (and later married one of his former pupils). He patiently demonstrated various skills, but they all proved beyond me – probably because I saw little point: I had no desire to join a football or cricket team. He was more effective in training me in mathematics, taking me to 'O' level. He amused the class on one occasion with what must have been an old joke. Teaching us the maths of compound interest, he drew our attention to an example in the textbook, beginning 'A man invests fifty pounds...', and, looking at one giggly girl in the middle of the classroom, quipped: 'At mention of a man invests, Wendy's breath comes in short pants.' Ho, ho, ho!

Eric Hill, who replaced Henry Treece following his retirement to concentrate on writing, did his best to explain to me what literature was about – but he disappointed me in being unable to explain English idioms. Only much later did I appreciate that most teachers of language-based subjects are really attracted to the study and enjoyment of the *written* word, and the teaching of language is a specialised pursuit that many experts on literature and culture regard with disdain.

Among the women teachers, I remember my first class teacher, Miss Cook, not formally qualified but brought in during the Second World War and capable of teaching geography and other subjects to the lower forms. Miss Raby ('Anna' or 'Banner', or even 'Banna': her nickname was never written down) drove to school from Goxhill in her Morris Minor (the original model, with the split windscreen), was enthusiastic in a bubbly sort of way, and was distinguished by having spent a year teaching in the United States (and demonstrated that fact by deploying her fork alone – rather than both knife and fork – when she was on lunch supervision duty). By contrast, Miss Procter – one of a small number of teachers with a Master's degree – was an altogether serious historian who found it difficult to control a class. She attempted to make it dramatically interesting by reading from a novel about Sir Francis Drake. 'Cacafuego! Cacafuego!', she shouted at the point when a hostile Spanish vessel of that name was sighted. We collapsed into giggles. On one occasion, she came into class and discovered that unpleasant-smelling fertiliser had been sprinkled on her desk by the son of a farmer, with the connivance of a group of other boys. I imagine she hated the job.

Miss Pollard joined the French department in 1955 and for several years continued what Billo had started. I learned much from her, and can still see her standing at the front of one of the classrooms in Baysgarth House, explaining the subjunctive or the *passé composé*, or the distinction between 'celui-ci' and 'celui-là'. On one occasion I was disappointed to be pipped to a prize of a bar of chocolate that she gave unannounced for the recitation of 'The Crow and the Fox' in La Fontaine's version of the Aesop fable. There was also Miss Bricknell, blonde and curvy, who taught lower-school geography and English, if I recall correctly, and left after three years for Germany apparently in search of a husband. And my second-form class teacher, Miss Smith, blonde and beautiful, who taught domestic science: even at the age of 12 I thought I fancied her – whatever that meant. There was a steady turnover among staff over the years, some arriving for twelve months before moving on to greener pastures. A number of them never taught a class that I was in, so they made little impression on me, although a certain Mr Parry struggled for a year to present Byron to a class with which he seemed to have little empathy.

Norman Goddard, the headmaster, was a linguist by training, and an accomplished pianist. Musically – and probably in other ways – a bit of a snob, he sneered perceptibly when one hapless girl confessed that the instrument she was learning was the piano accordion. In the second form, he taught us elementary Latin, in the days when that language was taught by paradigms: *porto, portas, portat, portamus, portatis, portant* (our textbook's variant on the usual *amo, amas, amat*). This method has become unfashionable, but I am convinced that it can be an effective and enjoyable way of learning a language. Chanting out the cases of nouns and adjectives or conjugating verbs is actually fun for children of a certain age. It certainly helped me understand how Indo-European languages function, by introducing inflexion and parts of speech that we had not encountered in our study of English or French. It was a method that I used for learning Russian after I left the grammar school, and other languages that I have dabbled in subsequently. Latin still helps me with English spelling, and it came in useful, along with French, when I lived as a research student in the Romanian-speaking Soviet republic of Moldavia – Romanian being the Romance language least developed from Latin. It was even more directly useful four decades after my last Latin lesson, when I was called upon as a Proctor to participate in the conferment ceremonies at Trinity College, Dublin, an old university that still confers degrees in the ancient language of scholarship.

Mr Goddard sometimes came across as something of a bully: he could impose orderly behaviour by twisting a pupil's ear, or tapping them hard on the skull with his knuckle, behaviour that would now not be allowed. He insisted on discipline throughout the school, including neat clothing and well-controlled hair styles. He once admonished the whole school: 'Your clothes may not be new, but there is no reason why they should not be clean.' More than one boy was ticked off and told to get a haircut – something that a football fan had once said to *him* during a match that he was refereeing. He must have been exasperated as fifteen- and sixteen-year-olds adopted the 'Tony Curtis' style: long at the back and combed into a 'D–A', then combed up from the sides and fashioned with Brylcreem to trail down on to the forehead in two curls that met in the centre. It was the time of 'Teddy Boys', and some pupils turned up to school in 'drainpipe' trousers – far from the regulation grey flannel – and crepe-soled shoes popularly known as 'beetle-crushers', 'brothel-creepers' or, elsewhere in the country, 'Wigan Palais stompers'.

For disciplinary offences, teachers and prefects would customarily require miscreants to write fifty or a hundred lines, to be written out and delivered the next day:

I must not talk in class.
I must not talk in class.
I must not talk in class.

or

I must not drop litter.
I must not drop litter.
I must not drop litter.

Persistent offenders, or those charged with more serious offences, were required to 'Stand under the clock' – the school's main timepiece, in the vestibule (the 'crush hall') outside the main hall, from which the staff rooms and the headmaster's office led. Standing under the clock, any delinquent pupil was automatically seen by Mr Goddard as he returned to school after lunch, and he dealt with the misdemeanour as he deemed appropriate.

THE SIGN OF AUTHORITY:
MY PREFECT'S BADGE

Serious disciplinary offences could be handled by the administration of a blow to the hand with a cane. This had been a common practice in Fanny Adamson's classroom in Immingham junior school, but now the law appeared to have changed: the punishment was formally witnessed by another member of staff, and the occasion marked in an official record book maintained for the purpose. Still rather a goody-goody myself, I was not subjected to this ultimate disciplinary measure (perhaps my Methodist upbringing made me deferential towards authority, or I was simply scared of the pain or the indignity, or afraid of having to explain to my parents); but as a prefect in my last year I certainly sent a few delinquents, as I saw them, to stand under the clock.

Timetabling and other constraints meant that we had to give up subjects at certain critical times in our careers. After a year of technical drawing and two years of woodwork – during which I made a small wall cupboard (a development permitted only to those whose door, with its mortise-and-tenon joints, ended up square and flat) and a little book-rest, with *fleur-de-lys* end-pieces, reflecting my passion for the Scouts at the time – I had to cease practical subjects. At 15, I surrendered biology and geography in favour of 'O' level physics and chemistry, an option that was available only every second year. I learned about the cooling curve for water, gravity and friction, magnetism and electricity from Freddie Manning, and from 'Horace' Hopley the theory of valency, how to read a chemical formula or equation, and various techniques for identifying substances – colour, litmus tests, flame tests, iodine tests, and so forth. Decades later I impressed a scientist by revealing that I knew the colour difference between brown ferric and green ferrous compounds. Freddie, a quietly spoken, somewhat dour Geordie, exuded a weariness derived from decades of trying to teach physics to pupils who found science beyond them. 'I've seen it all before', he would moan, in a voice somewhere between normal speech and *sotto voce*. 'Floods of tears when it comes to the School Certif' – he had evidently not registered the switch to 'O' and 'A' levels.

Mathematics continued until 'O' level, and I seem to have had some aptitude for the subject. Geometry, trigonometry and algebra all fascinated me, and I knew by heart two ways of proving Pythagoras' theorem about the square on the hypotenuse (probably not now, though!). I understood how to use logs and to calculate angles and areas and sides of triangles, rectangles and polygons. What's more, I could even see some ways of applying this knowledge to everyday problems – I saw the *point* of maths as I never saw it in the study of literature: with a knowledge of geometry, for example, it is possible to calculate how much carpet is needed to cover a floor even of an oddly-shaped room. It was with some disappointment that I had to drop maths after 'O' level. My passion for languages had the down side of having to study literature; but opting for science in order to pursue maths (and also to take some German, which I wanted to do) would have meant taking my weaker subjects. It was a difficult choice. Freddie, the physics master, said to my parents: 'He would make a scientist' – and I would certainly have made a better scientist than a litterateur. Fortunately, as my subsequent career developed, I did not need to make that choice.

I was sorry never to have proceeded as far as calculus in maths, although an opportunity came later in my career to study and use statistics. But we make our choices and have to live with them. Unable to choose between English and history (in which I had my lowest grades at

MYSELF (*seated left*) WITH LOWER-SIXTH SCIENCE FRIENDS, 1 JUNE 1960

'O' level), I started off with four subjects for 'A' level: French, Latin, English and History. But the quantity of reading was just too much for me, particularly as I still had some interests outside school, the Scouts and music (although I soon drifted away from the music group). Before Christmas, I decided to drop history – looking back I think that may have been a mistake, given the direction of my subsequent career. I slogged away at studying literature, sometimes starting my homework after supper at 7 o'clock, concentrating fiercely but getting nowhere until 9 or 9.30, and staying up until 1 a.m. to finish an essay for handing in the next day. That was a frequent pattern to my working life, and it made me wonder whether there was any truth in the old wives' tale that we are most alert one hour either side of the moment of our birth (I arrived soon after midnight). Be that as it may, I was never a morning person; my mind cranks up quite slowly, but if the ideas are flowing I can work late. This was the kind of thing one discovered about oneself in the Sixth Form of B.G.S. – a valuable lesson for life, along with many others.

By then, in 1960, my last year in the school, I had been made a Senior Prefect and Head Boy. We pupils never knew on what grounds prefects were selected, let alone the reasons for the choice of Head Boy and Head Girl. Was it the prerogative of the

Headmaster alone? Did he confer with other members of staff? What factors about the individuals were considered in the selection process? When I heard that I was to be appointed to this position, at the end of my year in the Lower Sixth, I didn't ask these questions. I was honoured, and pleased; but looking back I cannot see why I was chosen over others in the year. There was certainly no poll of pupils, not among my colleagues in the Lower Sixth, and even less among the whole school. Had that been the criterion, I'm sure other classmates were more popular than I was. After all, my contribution to school life was one-dimensional: I had a good academic record. But I had never represented the school in a sports team, or participated in any of the clubs that had been set up to offer other activities. My own extra-curricular activities had been outside the school, based in Immingham, mainly because transport from Barton after school hours was difficult to arrange in an era when very few families had cars. Occasionally, in the upper forms, I would go to school on my bike, and this gave me flexibility to take part in some activities after school (such as attending Christmas parties). But mainly B.G.S. was for instruction; my social life was based in Immingham. So it was not obvious why I was selected for this particular honour.

Neither, looking back, can I say my year as Head Boy was one of great distinction. Perhaps because my father always drummed into me the Christian virtue of humility, I was never allowed to get above my station, as he would have put it. Certainly, I would give 'lines' to junior pupils who infringed elements of the school's code of discipline; sometimes I would require an unruly boy pupil to pick up litter from the playing fields (and arrogantly accompany him as he did so). I also occasionally gave a sharp tap on the head to a noisy brat in the boys' changing room – much as prefects had done to me in the junior classes. But I always felt ambivalent about the wielding of authority, partly, I suspect, because it was never clear what authority I possessed or the purpose for which I was expected to use it. Were the prefects an adjunct to the school's disciplinary system? Undoubtedly. Were they supposed in some way to represent the pupils? Not so far as we could judge. Were they, as 'senior' pupils who had ostensibly been given a measure of responsibility, seen as a group that might have ideas about matters concerning how the school was administered? Most unlikely, as I discovered when I ventured to express the prefects' views about a proposed modification of the uniform and was effectively told that it was none of our business. I can think of no instance when, as Head Boy or as a prefect, I was 'consulted' about a school matter. Perhaps this uncertainty about what my formal role entailed explains the opinion that Miss Carr, as senior mistress, once expressed to my parents in a half-yearly report during my final year: 'He is a back-room boy rather than a leader in the field.'

Whether or not that is accurate, for me the principal event of the year was the vote of thanks that was offered to Dr Ethel Kirk, chairman of the governors, at the end of the proceedings on the annual Speech Day, before the customary singing of the national anthem. The speech was given in alternate years by the Head Girl and the Head Boy, and in 1960 it fell to me to make the speech.

I thought about it for some time. I had practically no experience of public speaking: the closest I had come to speaking to an audience was as the lead singer of the skiffle group in which I performed. I was certainly not a skilled orator or accomplished debater. I didn't want to make the speech either bland or pompous. I wanted a little humour, if possible. I knew that the general thrust was to thank Dr Kirk and her team, on behalf of the whole school, for the unpaid effort that they had put in over a number of years. And that year there was a success to be celebrated.

To the left of the main entrance, below the tennis courts, there was a garden bed that had been used by the grounds staff to grow vegetables for the school kitchen. It was affectionately known as 'the cabbage patch'. The school was always short of space. It had taken over Baysgarth House, which had served as a rather pleasant annexe for a number of years. But that was mere improvisation. Halfway through my career in the school, a new physics lab had been added; but that had not transformed the position. Further accommodation – for teaching, for changing before and after sports, for staff use – was still desperately required. By early 1960, the county council had authorised the construction of a new block of classrooms, to be located on the only available plot, and construction had commenced that autumn. That was something to be commented on, so it would become the positive note, and the humorous note, in my speech. But I was not allowed to deliver it without having it vetted by the Senior Mistress, Miss Carr (who had by then acquired the nickname of 'Dulcie', leading a pupil from a year above mine one Christmas to a scrawl on a blackboard in Baysgarth House: 'In Dulcie you Billo' – which I'm sure was merely a pun, with no aspersions being cast about either Billo or Dulcie).

'Madam Chairman,' I began. 'It is my honourable duty' (or words to that effect) 'to propose a vote of thanks to you and your committee of governors for all the effort you have put in for many years on behalf of Barton Grammar School. We know you have campaigned tirelessly for new classrooms, so that we can avoid the trek up and down Caistor Road to Baysgarth. And now we can see the fruits of your efforts rising on the cabbage patch.' As I hoped, this raised a smile on the face of Dr Kirk as she peered at me over her glasses. After a couple of sentences saying how much we should all miss Baysgarth House, I concluded my one-minute speech with a call to the school for three cheers for Dr Kirk, and the choir led us all into the school song.

The annexe rose rapidly – and in fact, unlike the rest of the school, it is still standing: an unlovely, cheap and nasty, two-storey 1960s eyesore, completely out of character with the rest of the school. The physics lab had been designed to blend in – mercifully, given its location on the 'inside' of one of the wings. I'm sure that the new block was a far more comfortable building to teach and study in than the makeshift classrooms that we loved down in the grand house in Baysgarth Park. The eighteenth-century moulded cornices and handsome shutters; the nineteenth-century grand staircase; the oak panelling, stained-glass window and elegant carved fireplace in the Sixth-Form Library, where we exchanged banter as we studied in 'free' periods: the beautiful oriel window in an upstairs classroom (for safety reasons we were forbidden to sit on its ledge, although, following Henry Treece – in fact, even without his example – we did so): this was not something that would be replicated in a purpose-built classroom block in the 1960s. Future generations of Bartonians would be spared running the springtime gauntlet of nesting rooks in the horse chestnut trees inside the gates of Baysgarth Park. But those who experienced the house were left with a residue of fond memories that a brutally functional modern building, however well-appointed and equipped, cannot match.

The event represented the end of an era for B.G.S., and in the school magazine *The Bartonian* of that year, more than one pupil used poetry and prose to express their emotions at the impending transfer. One poem bemoaned the loss of views of the park in favour of straight lines and symmetrical rooms', while a satirist – my classmate Marilyn Ellis, who had a wonderfully droll sense of humour – offered 'three cheers for engineering' as the school said goodbye to loose floorboards and creaking

THE BEAUTIFUL
ORIEL WINDOW
and
SIXTH-FORM
LIBRARY
(below)

stairs. I mean no disrespect to Dr Kirk and her team of governors, who were of course not responsible for the design, but I am thankful that I was never taught in it.

6

Skiffle, Blues, Beethoven, and All That Jazz

Most people over the age of 55 or so remember precisely where they were when they heard of the assassination of President John Kennedy in 1963 (I was in Leeds University, and went to the crowded Union building to watch the nine o'clock news). Younger people remember the assassination of John Lennon in 1980 or the death of Elvis Presley three years earlier. Very many also remember the death of Diana, Princess of Wales. A similar occasion in my life was 4 February 1959. I had just got on the school bus to B.G.S., when another pupil told me that Buddy Holly had died in a plane crash the previous day. I was shocked. Even more shocked when I saw a headline in that week's *Melody Maker* or *New Musical Express* (I forget which), that a classmate on the bus had brought with her: 'It's Buddy Without His Buddies' – and the story was about how Buddy Holly was about to go solo, without his backing group, The Crickets. The bitter irony was not lost on us teenagers, and we philosophically commented that 'it might be for the best': we could hardly imagine Buddy without his group. The superstitious poignancy came a few weeks later when his last recorded song, 'It Doesn't Matter Anymore', was released.

As a teenager, I came late to this kind of music. 'Pop' was not part of my household, except through the radio. With the arrival of John Sowerby to live in Immingham that changed.

It must have been in about 1957 – I remember being well into my secondary school, perhaps already fourteen, or approaching my four-teenth birthday. Sowerby moved to Immingham from Gainsborough, in the west of the county. His father had died a year or two earlier and his mother had just remarried, to the very popular vicar of St. Andrew's church, the Reverend John Moon, who used to do his rounds in the village on a 125cc BSA Bantam motorbike. John and his younger brothers lived in our street while the new vicarage was being built, and joined us at play.

There was already an established group of boys who hung about together: playing ball games on the green, riding their bikes around the streets, roller skating on the pavements, and in 1952 – the year of the Helsinki Olympic Games – running endlessly round the green, vainly dreaming of taking part in the 1956 Games in Melbourne. It was a new estate of council houses, populated by newcomers, including some from London who were being relocated as part of the policy of depopulating the sprawling, bomb-damaged capital. Most were young couples with families, whose children formed bonds in primary school, and went on to form different bonds in their various secondary schools. Outsiders found it hard to break in.

John Sowerby arrived one weekend, and was no doubt sent with his bike to attach himself to the three or four locals who were out playing. We were initially not impressed. It turned out that he would be going to the same school as me and one or two others on the street – B.G.S. – so there was some reason for getting to know him. But he struck us by his lack of chin, his effete button-down collars (none of us ever wore those), his feeble jokes about the names of classical composers – 'Bake-oven' for Beethoven; 'Rips-her-corsets-off' for the well-known Russian composer; his even feebler Latin–English pun (possibly not even his original): *Caesar adsum jam forte*, which didn't work on us since B.G.S. Latin used *i* rather than *j*; and his pretentious use of sweat bands on his wrists for running, since athletic he was not. Yet he persevered, and he was accepted into the group. And since he was a neighbour I suppose I felt mildly responsible to make his acquaintance, not realising that he would become my best friend for a few years.

He was not academically brilliant, nor was he good at sport and games, but he turned out to have a natural musical talent. With no formal training, he played piano by ear – I particularly remember his version of what was to me the finger-breaking tune 'Zambezi' – and when skiffle became briefly popular, John Sowerby took to it with enthusiasm. Skiffle was a British version of music produced in the southern United States, songs sung to the accompaniment of guitars and banjos augmented by home-made instruments or even kitchen utensils adapted to produced notes – jugs, for example, blown across the opening to produce a bass sound. It was pioneered by the self-styled 'King of Skiffle', Lonnie Donegan, whose recording of 'Rock Island Line' with Chris Barber's Jazz Band had started the craze.

Perhaps in compensation for the loss of his father, John Sowerby's mother seemed to indulge him in ways in which my parents could not afford to entertain my brother and me. He was given a guitar, a mass-produced item bought by mail order from the army surplus Headquarter & General Supplies, on which thousands of would-be Lonnie Donegans learned to strum their first chords. With the aid of Bert Weedon's *Play in a Day – Guide to Modern Guitar Playing*, he quickly learned a few chords, and persuaded some of his classmates to form a skiffle group.

Apart from Lonnie Donegan, there were many imitators whom in turn *we* could imitate. The Chas McDevitt skiffle group, featuring Nancy Whisky on 'Freight Train'; Johnny Duncan and his Blue Grass Boys ('Last Train to San Fernando'); the Vipers Skiffle Group ('Streamline Train' and 'Railroad, Steamboat') – all stimulated our ambitions as we listened for half an hour on Saturday mornings to 'Saturday Skiffle Club', introduced by Brian Matthew on the BBC Light Programme. When it expanded to two hours of 'Saturday Club' to embrace pop and jazz (which purportedly came from a cellar – how many listeners were fooled?), our mothers were not pleased: teenagers under their feet all Saturday morning, lounging around listening to the radio, was not what busy housewives needed. For the moment, though, we were happy to embrace the improvised music of our skiffle heroes.

We acquired a tea chest, upturned it, fixed a stout string to the centre of what was now its top and the other end to a broom handle, with which to add tension to the string, and this served as a double bass: at least it gave out a suitably deep thunk-thunk sound to underpin the basic rhythm. The 'instrument' was proudly painted with the name 'Pelham Skiffle Group', after Pelham Road, the main street in the village, where the vicarage was located, and where we practised. Keith Glover, a classmate, managed a passable performance on this home-made instrument. Charles Mingus he wasn't, nor Willie Dixon or Milt Hinton, but he could certainly hold a rhythm, evoke a range of 'notes' by adjusting the tension of the broom handle, and even fake the sound of bowing – at least to an undiscriminating ear listening mainly to the vocalist or lead guitar – by rapidly plucking with all four fingers of the right hand.

More subtle and complex rhythms were offered by the prestidigitations of the washboard player. Even in our under-equipped households, washboards were no longer a part of the weekly laundry ritual, but they could be easily bought for a few shillings. A piece of corrugated galvanised iron sheet held firmly in a wooden frame could be made to emit a satisfying rasp by scraping across the grooves of the metal, or a complex rhythm of clicks by tapping with the finger ends, encased in metal thimbles: not as subtle as tabla players, but cheaper than a drum kit. This was my instrument, and I remember the occasion when, accompanied by my mother (who knew about these things), I went to a haberdasher's ten miles away in Grimsby to buy a full set of new thimbles for a 'performance' at a dance in the village of East Halton.

With John Sowerby on lead guitar, Keith Glover on tea-chest bass and myself on washboard – joined by a succession of other classmates on various instruments – we practised for hours in John's bedroom, and later in the vicarage garage, every evening after finishing our homework. Occasionally – very occasionally – we would be engaged for what we called a 'booking': a half-hour stint in a village hall, while the jazz band or DJ took a break. We would lug our instruments – sometimes on public transport, since cars were not part of our life – to these venues, wait anxiously for our scheduled time, clamber on to the stage and perform, probably with more enthusiasm than musicality. Initially, everything was acoustic, so we had no need to set up equipment; later John (by this time, we had nicknamed him 'Philbert', abbreviated to 'Phil'), attached a pickup and plugged his newly electrified guitar into a cheap amplifier. Who did the singing? Hard to remember, but I imagine we all did. I sat at the back of the stage, washboard on my lap, fingers tapping and scraping the thimbles across the 'instrument', working to a frenzy in our finale, an imitation of Lonnie Donegan's 'Gambling Man', when for dramatic effect I would deliberately let the thimbles fly off my fingers. Health and Safety matters didn't come into it in those days. Today, I might end up in court.

Our repertoire consisted of all the songs that we heard on record or on the radio, with Lonnie Donegan's latest hits quickly absorbed, the words scribbled down, sometimes taken from the sheet music but more often from a weekly magazine that printed the words of the latest hit songs (but, possibly for copyright reasons, sometimes inaccurately transcribed).

So much did this hobby engage us, and so successful did we seem –

always hoping to be 'discovered', although we had no clue how that might happen – that John's mother bought him a drum kit. Actually, that's a bit of an exaggeration: a snare drum followed later by a cymbal and a hi-hat. 'Phil' quickly mastered these, and it looked as though my services on the washboard would shortly be no longer required. And so it turned out: I was encouraged to switch to the drum, so I continued as the percussion section of the group, and we changed our name – and the paintwork on the tea-chest bass – to 'Black Diamonds'. We continued in that configuration for a few months, perhaps a year and a half.

I was, I concede, not much of a drummer – but since those days I have retained an interest in percussionists: Gene Krupa, Buddy Rich, Max Roach and other greats of jazz, and in the backing of popular groups. But my lack of talent, if not of a genuine feeling of rhythm, and soaring ambition persuaded me to aim for the front row: I wanted a guitar.

Buying even such a crude, plywood instrument as 'Phil' possessed was beyond the range of my modest pocket money, but I was keen. One Saturday afternoon in January 1958 I happened to be in Grimsby for my fortnightly haircut. On my way back to the bus station, I wandered past a junk shop where I spotted a battered guitar in the window. This sight distracted me from the itching caused by snippets of hair inside my collar. The instrument was sprayed dark blue or black, and had the steel strings and narrow fingerboard of a jazz guitar. It must have been played for years in smoky bars and clubs, and its former owner had evidently decided that its days as the instrument of a serious performer were over. I was tempted – but not quite enough. The asking price of thirty shillings (£1.50) seemed a little steep, and in any case I didn't carry that amount of cash. It represented several weeks' pocket money. But I went home and thought about it, counted my savings and made some calculations.

Two weeks later, when I returned to town for another short-back-and-sides, the guitar remained in the window, having gathered a little more dust, but still I couldn't decide. It looked pretty forlorn, its paintwork badly scratched, a couple of strings missing, its tuning keys a bit rusty. I again went home empty-handed. I fretted over it for the rest of the weekend and made my decision. I headed off on the school bus on the Monday, having given my brother a green one-pound note and a brown one for ten shillings to take to school in the opposite direction to mine, with instructions to buy the guitar. I was overwhelmed when he came home with it – and he had knocked down the price to one pound! The junk shop owner must have despaired of selling it otherwise.

Then began the work of making it playable again. Off came the bridge and the tail-piece that held the strings to the body behind the bridge. I removed the rusty chrome tuning keys. I carefully scraped all the paint from the body and neck, and recast it in natural French polish, which I mixed myself from methylated spirits, shellac and linseed oil – something I had learnt from my grandfather. Day after day I applied a coat of polish, carefully and conscientiously rubbing down with the finest sandpaper before beginning the task. I bought and fitted a set of new brass tuning keys, and reassembled the instrument, finishing it off with a fairly crude plectrum guard, cut out of linoleum and painted black, that vaguely matched that of my idol, Lonnie Donegan. Not entirely satisfied, I later fitted a Spanish guitar bridge, doing away with the tail-piece. My mother, a genius with a sewing machine, made me a carrying case in blue cloth, with red piping and a zip fastener: I still possess both guitar and cover.

THE BLACK DIAMONDS SKIFFLE GROUP, 1958
JOHN SOWERBY RONALD HILL KEITH GLOVER

Thus re-kitted, I steadily expanded on the three chords that I had learnt to play on Phil's instrument, persuaded my fellow artistes that I could play rhythm guitar, and we found someone else to bash the drum and cymbal. My ambition drove me yet further, and I more or less imposed myself as lead singer, accompanying myself on rhythm guitar and occasionally banjo, also borrowed from Phil's collection of instruments, tuned and strummed like a guitar, according to whichever instrument Lonnie Donegan preferred on his recordings: banjo for 'Putting on the Style' and 'Does Your Chewing Gum Lose its Flavour on the Bedpost Overnight?', guitar for almost everything else.

To say that Lonnie Donegan was our hero would be to understate the slavish intensity with which we followed him. Practically every song, every inflection, every nuance of interpretation was copied from him. And I was oh, so flattered, when after a rehearsal for a 'performance' at one of the school Christmas parties a friend observed that he thought I looked like Lonnie as the curtain opened. So devoted was I that I even affected the name 'Lonnie Collin' – displaying my erudition, since my stage surname was derived from the French *colline*, meaning 'hill'. We B.G.S. boys were so clever!

We continued to practise, week in, week out. We had the occasional 'booking' and earned a bit of pocket money. There were also periodical changes in personnel. Two or three individuals performed on drums, the last (and no doubt best) being Terry ('Tetley') Parkin, and a succession of rhythm guitarists including Malcolm ('Aloysius' – 'Al' – or mysteriously 'Dad') Kicks, and Roy ('Spit' or 'Goz') Spittlehouse. We all took it very seriously. Arguments flared over missed beats or bum notes, or over whether our copy of an original actually played the identical notes. We sought new songs for our repertoire, expanding beyond skiffle and American folk to the pop of Buddy Holly ('Peggy Sue', 'That'll Be the Day'), added the occasional instrumental piece (Philbert once performed on piano in public, to my inept guitar accompaniment – someone commented a couple of days later that it sounded as though I had been tuning up), and even composed our own pretty feeble tunes.

As time went by, girlfriends, with their accompanying jealousies, started getting in the way of our diligent practising, and preparations for 'O' level exams disrupted our routine in the spring of 1959. There was never any serious bust-up, but we rather drifted apart – the story even of many professional pop bands over the decades. Some of us left school at sixteen, while I went on to do 'A' levels. I dropped out, and, under various names, the group continued for a while; some members lasted in various bands in the area for several years – The Wasps and The Echoes – and even performed alongside national stars in various locations. From little acorns ...

Sadly, John 'Philbert' Sowerby contracted an unnamed debilitating disease soon after leaving school. He suffered double vision and loss of muscle power and was taking various tablets for his condition. He was obliged to give up his job. He steadily deteriorated, while still struggling to play music, and he died at the age of barely eighteen in early 1961. It was the first death of a friend I had ever experienced, and it coincided with the retirement of Mrs Wilson, the superintendent of the kitchen that prepared lunches in B.G.S. Some of my school friends thought my overbearing sadness was at the departure of the long-standing fixture in the kitchen. Alas, my mind was on other things, and a group of us took a day off school the following week to attend Phil's funeral.

'Philbert' and I were no longer close friends by that stage, but I felt bereft. I knew he had altered my life. He had opened my ears to a whole range of new musical influences, very different indeed from the *bel canto* singing of oratorios, opera arias and serious songs that I heard in our family home. I became fascinated by the blues and by American folk music, a fascination that has remained with me. For school prizes on two occasions I selected books on blues, and over the years I collected recordings by many of the great performers: Big Bill Broonzy, Blind Lemon Jefferson, Robert Johnson, John Lee Hooker, Muddy Waters, Lightnin' Hopkins – I loved them all (and still do).

For many years I carried in my mind a collection of American folk songs, 'America at Play', recorded in the 1950s by Guy Carawan and Peggy Seeger, that Philbert had bought second-hand and lent to me. It was probably already out of the catalogue by that stage, so sporadically in the ensuing years I made a point of browsing in used record shops in the hope of finding a copy, but without luck. Eventually, the Internet came to my rescue, and I managed to secure a copy of a CD transcription of the collection – 'American Ballads and Folk Songs' – from a company in Dorset. I play it now and then, and 'Philbert' returns to my mind: the cheap guitars, the hours of practice in the garage of the Immingham vicarage, the public performances, the girlfriends: it all comes vividly back, and with it my long-gone youth.

I also tried my hand at another skill: song-writing. Unlike Philbert, I had some formal musical training. In addition to 'down – window – corridor – up' in Fanny Adamson's class, I had a couple of years' piano tuition at the age of eleven or twelve, so I knew about time and key signatures, and I could read the notes and relate them to a keyboard. Alas, I had no talent for writing words, and even less for composing catchy tunes, so that 'career' was stillborn. A couple of songs that we performed to distinctly unimpressed audiences: that was all I could muster.

By that stage, though, my musical horizons had been widened enormously. Skiffle proved to be a passing fad, despite a bold assertion in a book at the time (written by a Church of England clergyman!) that it would continue. It was a vulgar, commercialised blend of American blues and country music, packaged for a British audience, which at least had the merit of encouraging a generation of teenagers to take an interest in music making. Some – and I was one of them – also took a more profound interest in folk music and the blues, which also extended to jazz. The skiffle craze was preceded and followed by a brief flourishing of Traditional jazz, with Chris Barber, Acker Bilk, Kenny Ball, Humphrey Littleton and others enjoying popular success. One hit of the time was Humphrey Littleton's 'Bad Penny Blues', a tune that I still love, which was played by a talented jazz pianist in our class, Alan Dickinson, when several sixth-formers used to meet in one of the classrooms during the lunch hour. I started buying the odd jazz compilation of Dixieland, Mainstream and even Modern Jazz – and, again, I found I thoroughly enjoyed it. I would hardly say I *appreciated* it in the way a performer or genuine aficionado would. But I did feel that my mind was opened as it otherwise might never have been.

In fact, in my early teens I was considered quite 'square' in my tastes – indeed, with a bit of encouragement I might even have earned the nickname that one classmate gave to her father: 'Cube', because he was exceptionally 'square'. We then had no record player, so collecting and listening to records was not a hobby of ours. Dad was somewhat cloth-eared, and my mother's musical tastes were entirely high-brow, principally oratorio and songs with a religious theme, with a strong concern for singing *technique* rather than music in a wider sense. The limited opportunities for listening to pop were discouraged by my mother's dismissive comments about it. At school I was effectively excluded from conversations about popular culture, to the extent that, when one of the girls in my class asked me whether I liked Pat Boone, I asked innocently, 'Who is she?' John 'Phil' Sowerby's arrival changed all that.

The result is that my adult life has been enriched by an eclectic love of music of many genres, from plainsong to Penderecki, via Bach and Beethoven, Schubert and Shostakovich; from country blues and bottle-neck guitar to The Pentangle and Clannad; from Jelly Roll Morton, Louis Armstrong, Ella Fitzgerald and Duke Ellington to Oscar Peterson, Louis Stewart and the Modern Jazz Quartet. And I retained an abiding enthusiasm for the classic rock 'n roll years of 1956–60, the era of Little Richard, Eddie Cochran, Gene Vincent, and especially Buddy Holly. I also never lost a deep love of the guitar – the most intimate of instruments, as a soloist suggested at a concert that I once attended: the fingers are in direct contact with the string that makes the sound, with no keys, no tubes, no valves intervening. The harp possesses similar qualities; only the human voice is a more direct instrument. Julian Bream and John Williams have remained my heroes of the classical style, joined by many brilliant performers of a new generation and from unexpected parts of the world, including China. I appreciate the technical brilliance of many rock guitarists, the improvisatory genius of Django Reinhart and other jazz performers, the knife-edge playing of slide guitarists, the brilliant flourish of the flamenco style.

The radio was a good source of music in the absence of a record player. Apart from 'Saturday Skiffle Club' and then 'Saturday Club', I regularly listened to a half-hour programme on Saturday evenings: 'Guitar Club'. Introduced by the jazz guitarist Ken Sykora, it offered an eclectic range of guitarists and styles, including the calypso singer Cy Grant, the jazz performer Ike Isaacs, and the teenage wonder of the classical guitar, John Williams, recently arrived in London from Australia. When I met this world-class performer in Dublin, four and a half decades later, he was somewhat tickled to be reminded of those days, and he gleefully played the programme's signature tune for me.

My musical tastes were also set by what was played on radio around Sunday lunchtime. From noon, 'Two-Way Family Favourites' played requests for British troops in the occupation force in Germany and for their families back home. Sentimental songs of departure and separation appeared week after week: Ella Fitzgerald's classic performance of 'Every Time We Say Goodbye', Pat Boone's 'I'll Be Home', and Nana Mouskouri singing 'The White Rose of Athens'. These all lodged in my consciousness alongside the pop songs that changed week by week, including those by the 'king' (Elvis Presley), the Everly Brothers, Paul Anka and their British counterparts, including long-forgotten performers such as Al Saxon, Craig Douglas, Terry Dene and Edna Savage. After lunch, there was 'The Billy Cotton Band Show', which opened with the Cockney bandmaster shouting 'Wakey, wakey!' – to our Northern ears 'Wikey, wikey!' – at his lunch-laden listeners, featuring Alan Breeze singing novelty songs including one about a football referee, who 'went and lost his pea', so his 'little wooden whistle' wouldn't whistle. Billy Cotton himself entertained with a song about a lonely little petunia in an onion patch. Such novelty songs also featured on 'Children's Favourites' on Saturday morning when we were small – Max Bygraves singing a love song between two toothbrushes or one about a mouse in Amsterdam: instantly forgettable, unless you heard them week after week at an impressionable age.

The family acquired a decent record player in 1959 – not exactly hi-fi in the strictest sense, but at least one of the early stereo models, and from then on, as my schoolboy pocket money allowed, I slowly built up a collection of recorded music of all kinds. I managed to attend Lonnie Donegan concerts in Lincoln, Hull and Cleethorpes. It was later, as a student at Leeds University, that I explored a wider range of music and musicians in the flesh. Julian Bream, Memphis Slim and Bert Jansch at the university; John Williams and Yehudi Menuhin in concerts in the City Hall; at Harewood House, Norma Procter, the contralto born in Cleethorpes (a cousin of my history teacher); Polish jazz in a city-centre bar; Duke Ellington, Coleman Hawkins and Ella Fitzgerald in the Odeon Cinema, sitting in the gods a quarter of a mile from the stage, or so it seemed. In the same venue Chuck Berry, the Moody Blues, the Dave Clark Five, and even the Shadows (without, I think, Cliff Richard). All of this I regarded as part of my education just as much as seeing it as a form of entertainment and a way of meeting attractive young ladies.

I also joined the World Record Club, as a source of cheaper, and sometimes exclusive, recordings in the days of strict credit control and resale price maintenance (which prohibited price competition among retailers of most products). I steadily built up a collection of Beethoven symphonies, choral works, Mozart and Haydn concertos, jazz stars including Duke Ellington, Billy Strayhorn, Glen Miller and Coleman Hawkins, blues and folk music by Josh White, Sonny Terry, Memphis Slim and Ray Charles, all on the WRC label, expanded by records that I later bought on trips abroad when I began to travel. Since my first visit to Prague, in early December 1978, a Christmas morning ritual has been to play a recording that I obtained on that occasion of a Czech Christmas Mass, a joyous work by the composer Jakub Jan Ryba. In 1982, during a two-way coast-to-coast drive across the United States, I constantly listened on my car radio to country radio stations, whose tuneful and sentimental but undemanding music kept me company: Crystal Gayle, Alabama, The Bellamy Brothers, Juice Newton, Conway Twitty, Eddie Rabbitt, Dr. Hook – nowadays I cannot hear this kind of music without thinking of my drive through Laramie, Cheyenne, Fargo and other towns with cowboy country names.

I was particularly taken by a song by Eddie Rabbitt, which kept buzzing around my head for the next twenty years. I hadn't registered its title, and whenever I visited the States I would look at recordings by the singer in the hope that something would jog my memory. It never did. I remembered a couple of lines, but they carried not a hint about the name of the song: 'On a shelf behind a book' and 'In a closet on a hook' – not very promising. Eventually, the Internet came to my rescue, as it had with Guy Carawan and Peggy Seeger. A search engine revealed that the song had appeared on a particular album before its release as a single, and its title was 'I Don't Know Where to Start'. How could I get a copy of this? Again, the Internet rescued me. I discovered that it was available in a mail-order record store in the state of Oregon, and I placed an order online. Ten days later, the package arrived with the 45 r.p.m. disc inside. But this was no ordinary disc: it was a special pressing for radio stations, with the same song appearing on both sides, so that the DJ need not worry about getting it the right side up. It occurred to me that this might be the very record that I had heard over the airwaves in Montana, or Colorado, Kansas or wherever.

As a graduate student in the Soviet republic of Moldavia – where the predominant culture is Romanian – I made a point of attending symphony concerts, at which I heard some of the Soviet Union's distinguished and up-and-coming star soloists, including the violinists Leonid Kogan and Nelly Shkolnikova, and the pianist Nikolai Petrov. I also went to concerts of Romanian–Moldavian folk music and dance, and developed an abiding love of it: at times vibrant and vigorous, at others melancholic and wistful, with the characteristic instruments of the region – violin, cimbalom, panpipes and whistle (*fluier*) – and I bought LP recordings that still take me back almost half a century. On one memorable occasion I was astounded to hear a brilliant musician in Moldova play real tunes on a leaf from a lime tree – not the crudely whistled single note that most schoolboys learn to produce by blowing across a blade of grass held between the thumbs, but genuine Romanian dance tunes performed with great musical competence and finesse.

I continued to listen to the wireless, as we used to call it. Transistor radios had become widely available in the late 1950s, replacing the heavy valve-driven affairs that required a large battery that never gave service for more than a couple of hours. As a student, I bought a cheap little transistor, which had a woefully tinny sound that I found very unsatisfactory. But it was through that medium that I came across some of the world's great music. I remember in my second year as an undergraduate hearing a magnificent choral piece by Beethoven for the first time, and intuitively knowing it was his Choral Symphony – a wonderful work that I had been vaguely aware of. Once having heard it, I have been overwhelmed by its majesty and power ever since. The same tinny transistor first introduced me to Penderecki's 'Threnody for the Victims of Hiroshima', announced on the BBC Third Programme as 'Tren', which was performed twice, separated by a talk about the meaning of the music – a depiction of the atomic bomb attack on the Japanese city at the end of the Second World War. I would listen to Antony Hopkins on the Third Programme on Sunday afternoons, 'Talking About Music', with his wonderfully illuminating insights. And I listened to Indian music concerts on radio – to the extent that I could be quite dismissive of George Harrison's and other pop guitarists' embrace of the sitar, critical of the fashion for Indo-jazz fusion in the mid-sixties (although I bought a couple of LPs in that style, which I still find enjoyable: at heart I'm no purist), and enthusiastic about Ravi Shankar when he performed in the Hexagon restaurant at Essex University.

As a graduate student in that institution, I would amuse myself on weekend evenings by listening to one of the early pirate radios, Radio 390, anchored in the Thames estuary. There was a daily programme of rock 'n roll and a Sunday evening blues show, hosted by Mike Raven, who styled himself 'The oldest living teenager in captivity' (he was in his forties by then). It was all great fun, and I even exchanged a letter or two with him. After the closing of the pirate stations, he transferred to the BBC, but I myself had moved away. Many years later I discovered what an interesting character 'Mike Raven' was: ballet dancer, photographer, conjurer, interior decorator, sheep farmer, author, broadcaster – and an extremely knowledgeable and infectiously enthusiastic fan of blues and rock 'n roll.

I cannot imagine my life without music, and for that I am grateful for my mother's chromosomes. Perhaps she instilled a musical sense as she sang to me as a baby: not just lullabies and nursery rhymes, but the tuneful wartime country song, 'You Are My Sunshine'. Although I am a master of no instrument, and I would hardly call myself educated about music in any profound sense, my musical tastes remain very broad-ranging. I happily listen to all but the most avant-garde in jazz or the classical genre (and I would add much of modern 'pop', which strikes me as vacuous and tuneless, if sometimes pretentious). I retain a particular affection for the classical guitar, but am moved by Bach's solo cello suites, Beethoven's late string quartets, or Barber's 'Adagio for Strings', exhilarated by the exuberance of Schubert's 'Trout' Quintet, and enchanted by Tchaikovsky's 'Serenade for Strings'. Country music relaxes my mind, since it is both tuneful and essentially banal (Johnny Cash is one obvious exception). Modern rock performers excite me with their technical wizardry: Jimmy Hendrix, Carlos Santana, Marc Knopfler all leave me breathless. Traditional jazz is happy, Fats Waller is amusingly entertaining, Duke Ellington was a great composer by any standards, and modern jazz is very relaxing: the music of the Modern Jazz Quartet, unfashionable though it now is, still sounds cool and sophisticated to my ears, along with Bill Evans and Art Tatum. I thrill to Ike and Tina Turner's 'River Deep, Mountain High', produced by the recording genius Phil Spector, introduced to me by Mike Raven on Radio 390, and called the best pop record of all by one writer on the theme. The girl groups of the sixties – the Supremes, the Chiffons, the Ronettes, the Crystals – have a cachet of their own. Rock 'n roll from the 1950s takes me back to my teenage strumming and vocalising.

With advancing years and a developing aural palate, I now listen with a more critical ear to the crude recording quality, the triteness of many of the words (I refuse to call them 'lyrics' – the sheet music of the 1950s unpretentiously called them words), the aimlessness and careless phrasing of the performances by singers who seemed not to understand what they were singing about (and proved the point by grinning as they performed songs of sadness and tragedy), the sameness of the voices on the collections of hits from my teenage years. Some of them, I sometimes feel when I hear them today, were scarcely better than my own crude performances with the Black Diamonds, *nés* the Pelham Skiffle Group. But those performers *had* been 'discovered', whereas we hadn't, and that was all that mattered.

My own musical tastes moved on, outward and upward, and, unlike my fellow artistes from the 1950s, some of whom went on to enjoy success locally and farther afield, I would never have enjoyed any kind of career, even as an amateur, in pop music. The strange thing, though, is that I might never have listened to this range of music, which has been such a source of joy and pleasure over most of my lifetime, had it not been for the arrival at Immingham and B.G.S. of 'Philbert' Sowerby, who opened my ears and gave me the confidence to embrace different styles and types of music, and an appreciation of the versatile wonder of the guitar.

7

Diversion

Playing the washboard and guitar in the Black Diamonds added a welcome spice to life in an industrial village, which at the best of times was scarcely exciting. In the early 1950s very few families possessed a television set: the first on our street was installed – complete with the characteristic X-style aerial on the chimney stack – in time for the Queen's coronation on 2 June 1953. Every schoolchild in Lindsey had been given a copy of the New Testament, bound in a royal-blue cover with the royal coat-of-arms embossed in silver, to mark the occasion. The newspapers were full of editorials and advertisements greeting a 'new Elizabethan age' to replace the post-war period of austerity with optimism, underpinned by endless, almost free, nuclear electricity. On the happy morning of 2 June, after we had heard that Everest had been conquered a few days earlier by Edmund Hilary and 'Tiger' Tenzing, several families crowded into the Wright family's sitting-room, a couple of doors from where I lived, to witness the event, in black and white on a tiny screen. Across the county, my cousin Barry managed to take a photograph of Her Majesty on the throne, wearing the imperial crown of state and holding the orb and sceptre. Impressed as I was by the pageantry, and entertained, like the adults, by the magnificent figure of Queen Salote of Tonga, I did not understand how television works: I could not imagine that we were not watching a film of events that had taken place hours beforehand.

So long as I lived at home, there was no television set in the house, so my viewing took place in friends' homes. 'Six-Five Special', compèred by Josephine Douglas and Pete Murray and introduced by a signature tune performed with great energy by Don Lang and his Frantic Five, became a Saturday evening regular for the Black Diamonds. So, later, did 'Juke Box Jury', in which the suave David Jacobs played the latest record releases and invited a small panel of 'celebrities' to vote them a 'hit' (cue a buzzer) or a 'miss' (cue a raucous-sounding horn). Occasionally, visiting relatives or family friends, we would be allowed to see 'What's My Line', a panel game in which a team of regular 'television personalities' including Lady Isobel Barnet, Gilbert Harding, Barbara Kelly and the conjuror David Nixon would attempt to guess the occupation of a member of the public who mimed an action from his or her work. Those innocent days are a very distant memory in this era of hundreds of satellite channels and an Internet that provides all manner of innocent and not-so-innocent entertainment.

School itself offered some extra-curricular activities. Sports teams competed with other schools in the area on Saturday mornings. A chess club also engaged in inter-school competitions. The school had a choir, which performed at the Christmas carol service and on Speech Day in the autumn. Chad and his wife Edith set up a dancing club. A history society was formed, followed later by a sailing club. Plays were put on by the drama club, sometimes to considerable acclaim: 'Richard of Bordeaux', by Gordon Daviot, was a particular success in 1957. Circumstances made it difficult for those of us who lived as far away as Immingham to take part in these activities: public transport was non-existent after the departure of the school bus at 4 p.m., and cars were still far from common. Occasionally a teacher would give a lift home, but that could not be relied on – nor should it have been.

But most pupils managed to attend the Christmas parties, one for each year, and prefects usually attended those of the junior forms to give a hand. They were always preceded by a couple of weeks in which PT lessons and half an hour after lunch were devoted to trying to inculcate the rudiments of a few dance steps. The waltz most of us, even the most flat-footed, could manage. The Welsh barn dance, similarly, offered few serious demands, and it allowed every boy and girl to meet a variety of partners. The quickstep was a little more tricky. Performed to the accompaniment of a vinyl recording of Victor Sylvester and his orchestra, the basics proved accessible to most twelve-year-olds and upwards. However, when for some reason a different recording was used – identical rhythm, different tune – confusion ensued for many, including myself. Not a success – which was why the dancing club was started. On these occasions we would play the usual children's party games: musical chairs, pass the parcel, musical statues and others. A favourite was for all to attempt to put names to the photos posted around the hall of the prefects as babies. We would return home crammed into taxis, an opportunity as we grew older for half an hour's hand-holding or more familiar displays of affection.

To a great extent, back in North Lincs in the 1950s, most of the time we made our own entertainment, playing on the street. The metal wheels of cheap roller skates were worn out as we zoomed along the pavements. We rode our bikes, sometimes on lengthy trips for half a day or more in the Lincolnshire countryside – an activity that would be altogether too dangerous for twelve-year-olds today. We kicked a football across the grassy area in front of our houses, and in summer set up a wicket and played cricket. We would go into nearby fields and do the same, or we would climb the trees near the school on a bomb site that we called the Airy Mountain – and our school uniforms would come home smelling of the leaves of the balsam poplar trees.

After two or three years in the village, a few swings and a roundabout were installed in a field opposite the bottom of Princess Street, where a shopping centre now stands. These transformed summer evenings. After homework was completed, we were allowed to join other children from all parts of the village to use these facilities. There was no supervision, so boisterous adolescents and teenagers used the swings, and particularly the roundabout, in ways that would nowadays be regarded as quite dangerous. The whole facility would probably be closed today by 'Health and Safety'. We would swing with such energy that sometimes the user would be lying almost horizontal at the top of the arc. Some bold youths would show off by 'bailing out' – letting go of the supporting chains and flying into the air to land on the grass beyond, and hoping not to crash into another child. Smaller children running or walking behind or in front of the swing always posed a risk, and it is perhaps surprising that there were no serious mishaps. The roundabout was even more dangerous. Its rotation was induced by running round its concrete base, holding on to one of the iron tubing handles, and then leaping on. Seven, ten or even a dozen energetic teenagers could scramble on and off the device, spinning at considerable speed and risking falling as they leaped off, twisting their ankle, breaking an arm, or worse. Still, we found it great fun, and we got rid of excess energy, so I'm sure we slept well.

In the early summer, when the grass in the field was cut and left to dry out for hay, as the sweet scent of mown grass quickly dissipated the hay became another item for play. Boys (and girls) would romp in the drying grass, picking handfuls and stuffing it down the necks of their rivals. And adolescent couples would stroll off to a far corner, or into the nearby lane, for kisses, cuddles and perhaps more – but usually not very much more in those times of semi-innocence. 'Going all the way' was something that only 'bad girls' did (there was no mention of 'bad boys' in those days) – but a fair number of them and their boyfriends were believed to be willing to go quite some distance. 'Goodnight, Mary. Good luck, Jim' was a greeting overheard one sultry twilight evening.

Sometimes entertainment would be put on in what was affectionately known as the 'Tin Mish', in Immingham. This was a corrugated iron structure at the lower end of Pelham Road, near the old heart of the village, originally a mission hut for some Christian denomination or other – possibly the Missions to Seamen, which now had a building down at the dock. It served not only as a substitute village hall, but also as a 'ballroom of romance' for infrequent Saturday night dances (they were then called 'hops'; now they are 'gigs') and for weekly showings of films by a projectionist who toured village halls in a van with a large metal tube on the roof, containing a rolled-up screen. This was erected in the hall, and we would pay our sixpence to watch a grainy Western in the gloom.

On one occasion the programme of the 'Tin Mish' featured a performance by a man with a distinguished black beard and the equally distinguished name, Marcus, and his 'talking' dogs. After persuading his two Alsatians to perform various 'tricks', Marcus invited members of the audience to pose questions to the starring dog; these would be answered by a single bark for 'no' and two barks for 'yes'. It was All Fools' Day, 1 April, and one of my classmates asked whether the hound had played an April Fool's joke on his master. The dog cannot possibly, of course, have understood what the question was about, but he barked twice. So Marcus did some quick thinking to explain: that morning, the dog had come to Marcus in his caravan to indicate that there was someone at the door; it turned out there wasn't. 'April Fool!' woofed the dog. I'm not sure how many of the young audience were taken in, but we queued up afterwards to purchase publicity photos with the purple imprint of a dog's paw on them. I suspect I still possess mine, somewhere among my accumulated belongings.

Before the Pelham Skiffle Group and later the Black Diamonds, I became a keen Boy Scout. As in many other things, it was my younger brother John who introduced me to the 1st Killingholme Troop – a three-mile bike ride away. Every Thursday evening, whatever the season, we would cycle over to the Scout hut in the grounds of the house belonging to Cecil Reginald Victor Gardiner, the most unlikely Scoutmaster one could imagine. He was quite short, thin, gnarled and tanned, with spindly legs and knobbly knees, which he was quite happy, indeed proud, to display in his uniform (well, he was proud to wear the uniform). I discovered in my late teens that he had, as a young man, endured some minor brain surgery, which probably explains his childlike demeanour. He had inherited a certain sum, which was apparently controlled by trustees. He was still a boy at heart, and simply loved the company of the Scouts. There was never anything other than pride and affection in his relationship with the Troop. His existence revolved around the Scouts and playing the organ – badly – in the local Methodist chapel. As head of the troop, he was affectionately referred to as 'Skipper', shortened to 'Skip'.

Every week he would perform all the ritual of Scoutmaster, as envisaged by Baden-Powell, the movement's founder. The whole ethos was somewhat military, with uniforms, inspections, marches, flag ceremonies, church parades, salutes, and other elements of the military life, including camps, that earned the strong disapproval of my grandfather (although he uttered none of that in our presence).

At the start of the weekly meeting there would be a roll-call, and we were inspected for the neatness of our uniform, acquired piecemeal, as the pocket money allowed. It started with the bottle-green beret, to be worn with the badge over the left eye, the green garter tabs and the bright green neckerchief held at the neck by a 'woggle' – and I was proud to learn how to make a Turk's head woggle later in my Scouting career; it progressed to the shorts, shirt, epaulettes, badges and eventually lanyard. A thumb-stick came much later: a stout ash walking stick that reached to shoulder height, with a 'V' at the top end to accommodate the thumb and a brass ferrule and iron tip at its lower end.

After inspection, divided into patrols (mine was Peewit with, I think, a green-and-white shoulder tab), we would practise tying knots of various kinds: granny, reef, sheepshank (for shortening a rope), round turn and two half-hitches (for fastening a rope to a pole or fence), bowline (for something to do with sailing – but since I never sailed, I had no use for that). We learned 'whipping' (binding the cut end of a rope with heavy thread to prevent fraying) and splicing, a heavy-duty version of whipping performed by weaving the strands of the rope back on themselves, and also a way of joining two ropes securely by intertwining the cords. All very useful in the right context, but there was little call for any of these skills in the Scoutmaster's garden in Killingholme. Perhaps of greater use was the smattering of First Aid that we picked up, including how to stop a nose-bleed, or fit a splint to a broken limb and use a Scout neckerchief as a sling to support a splinted arm. It was in the Scouts, too, in preparation for my 'Handyman' badge, that I learned the right order in which to paint the elements of a panelled door: beading, panels, rails, stiles. It has a 'down – window – corridor – up' ring to it, but it's what the professionals do. From my grandfather I had learnt the importance of applying knotting to fresh pine before painting, otherwise the knots will permanently show through the paint. Later in my life I suffered for a quarter of a century after unwittingly employing an incompetent 'painter' who was unfamiliar with this practice.

I cannot honestly say that this knowledge has been of practical value in my subsequent career, but I believe that no training of the hand or mind is completely wasted, and the Scouts certainly offered an enjoyable way of spending a couple of hours one evening a week.

Even more enjoyable were the other activities that came with the Scouts. Apart from a few ropes and poles, the 1st Killingholme Troop had no equipment to speak of. It had no funding: the weekly subscription was perhaps sixpence (2.5p), which meant that less than a pound a week came into the kitty. When I became treasurer of the Troop after a couple of years I guarded it carefully. In any case Skip – my brother and I for some reason soon started calling him 'Porky' – had no organisational skills to buy tents, or facilities to store them. But through his involvement with the district Scouting authorities, he got to know the Ellis brothers, Jim, Ted and Ron, who ran the 3rd Grimsby Troop, a larger, better-organised and altogether more serious operation than ours. I rather suspect that the Ellis brothers took pity on Skip and indulged him for the sake of us boys, and we were allowed to take part in some of their activities, including camping.

My first night under canvas – apart from the occasional uncomfortable experience with John in our own tent on the back lawn – was one Easter weekend, when we joined the 3rd Grimsby at their own regular camping site. This had been arranged by Skip, and four of the 1st Killingholme Troop – or perhaps half a dozen – turned up on the bus, rucksacks bulging with bedding, clothing, enamel plate and mug, a knife, fork and spoon set, and whatever else we imagined we needed for a couple of nights in camp. Unfortunately, it had not been established that we possessed no tents of our own, and there were some expressions of dismay on the part of our hosts. Skip mumbled an apology, and the leaders of 3rd Grimsby graciously – but practically – found some way of allowing us to use one of their tents. Where Skip spent those two or three nights I don't remember – probably sharing with one or other of the very indulgent Ellis brothers – but we managed comfortably, survived the experience, and went home happy, having endured lumpy porridge, cooked 'dampers' (flour and water baked over the embers of a wood fire on the end of a stick – delicious when smothered in raspberry jam; dismal otherwise), practised building bridges with staves and ropes, and listened to an improvised sermon after Sunday lunch on Easter Day.

After I had been a member for a couple of years, the troop moved from Killingholme to Immingham, changing its name to 1st Immingham and acquiring a Cub section under the new headmaster of the primary school, Mr Mead. It also started a Senior Scout Troop, in which I led the 'Robert Falcon Scott' patrol. We also gained a new Scoutmaster, who worked at the local fire station, and Skip promoted himself to Group Master. Since we now had a new Skipper, Reg Gardiner chose himself a new title: 'Nomad', after the character whose Nature rambles, under the title 'Wandering with Nomad', entertained generations of young listeners to Children's Hour on the BBC Home Service. 'Nomad' now took something of a back seat in the Scout Group, trying to impress us by sitting at a desk, a portable typewriter in front of him, wandering around the weekly meeting, observing the various patrols at work, and making what he implied were notes in what purported to be shorthand. When we asked him what he had written, he would smile enigmatically and keep us guessing by politely indicating that it was none of our business.

Camping was always good fun, and I'm sure my parents – and those of other teenage boys – were happy to get rid of their offspring for a couple of days. We found two or three sites owned by friendly farmers who allowed the troop or a patrol to camp for a weekend. Each Scout was responsible for his own kit, including toiletries, which were packed into individual rucksacks. As leader of Peewit patrol, I used to insist that tin mugs should *not* be tied to the outside of the backpack: 'A Scout should not look like a Christmas tree.' On one occasion, as troop leader I was responsible for checking the kit, including tents (which by then we had managed to acquire), cooking pots, matches, toilet paper (vital, but easily overlooked!), and provisions. Alas, I forgot the sugar! I decided that improvisation was a good thing for a Scout, and declared that a dollop of jam could be substituted to sweeten the porridge. During the day, Ian Botham, the new Assistant Scoutmaster who was accompanying us (alas, not the famous cricketer of that name), went back to Immingham on his bike and returned with sugar, plus one or two other items that had been forgotten. By evening we could have sugar in our tea. This provoked a ribbing by some of the boys. To the tune of Alma Cogan's hit song, 'Sugartime', I was greeted with an appropriate new version:

> Jam in the morning, jam in the evening, sugar by supper time.

On other occasions, I would go off alone, pitch my tent, dig a fire pit and a latrine, and happily entertain myself for a couple of days, sometimes being visited by friends. On one such trip, after I had set up camp and walked a quarter of a mile to beg a bucketful of water from the farm pump, walked back and hung the canvas bucket on a fence (since, of course, it would not stand), I suffered the humiliation of turning round from my fire to discover a cow contentedly drinking my water.

The summer of 1957 proved to be a highlight in my Scouting career. In July, my parents happily sent us off to join the 3rd Grimsby on a week's camping trip at Youlbury, a Scouts' activity centre near Oxford. This was an exciting trip, taking us by train from Grimsby to King's Cross, a transfer to Paddington, and thence to Oxford and on to the camp by bus. We enjoyed a week of tent life, eating the usual lumpy and sometimes burnt porridge for breakfast, peeling potatoes ('spud-bashing') during the morning in preparation for lunch, practising our knots, improving our woodcraft, and enjoying sing-songs round the camp fire, along with other troops from different parts of the country, in the evenings. Each troop would put on an entertainment for the whole camp, evoking cheers if it passed muster, or, if it was judged below par, the punning jibe: 'Weak, weak; very, very weak – in fact, a fortnight!' We greeted one another with the left-hand shake – part of the folklore of the movement, derived from an incident when an African child offered his left hand to Baden-Powell – and used the three-finger salute as we raised the flag each morning.

There was a day visit to London, which included lunch in the famous Lyons Corner House, on The Strand near Trafalgar Square – the first time I had ever experienced this London institution; I think I went there a couple of times as an adult – and a boat trip on the Thames, past the Palace of Westminster, which I proudly photographed with my Kodak Brownie 127. (Later in my teens, when I took up photography as a hobby, I used the negatives from that London visit to practise contact printing; many of them still survive, much faded by the passage of time.)

The week at Youlbury was notable for another incident that I remember, although it was not in any sense traumatic. One of the boys from the 3rd Grimsby – I think his name was Bob – was somewhat precocious sexually, showing off his assets to other boys in the semi-privacy of the eight-man tents, and reportedly demonstrating his prowess by using it to lift a kit bag (presumably not a fully laden one, though). Not that I witnessed this feat: I was too shy, or perhaps self-absorbed, to stray beyond my own tent, where I lay reading in the afternoon on my plastic air-bed – a present from my mother, bought by mail order, I suspect – which was promptly punctured with a small hole and proved difficult to sleep on through a whole night. I was somewhat shocked one day in the second half of the week to be approached by Bob and asked if he might masturbate me (although he used a vernacular phrase). I knew nothing of homosexuality at that stage; the word 'gay' had not acquired its current meaning, and I had never even heard the other crude euphemisms of the time. I was certainly not interested in being played with by another fourteen-year-old, if only because 'A Scout is clean in thought, word and deed', so I politely, if shyly, declined, and nothing more was heard of the proposition.

I imagine we were pleased to return home to Immingham at the end of the trip, but later that summer there was another great Scouting occasion. The World Jamboree which, in the golden jubilee year that marked the half-century since the publication of Baden-Powell's *Scouting for Boys*, was held at Sutton Coldfield in what was proudly referred to as the heart of England. I joined a special train from Grimsby for a day's visit, during which I was happy to show off my knowledge of French, advertised by my 'Interpreter' badge on my sleeve, and to take lots more photos.

In the following year, on 27 July 1958, the troop proudly turned up on parade to salute the Queen as she passed through Immingham. She had been in Scunthorpe and was to board the royal yacht, *Britannia*, at Immingham dock to spend the night before a visit to Grimsby. We locals had been amused, several weeks earlier, to hear the route from Scunthorpe announced on the BBC radio news. 'Scunthorpe; Winteringham; Barton-upon-Humber; Barrow-on-Humber; East Halton, Killingholme' – all this was fine, even if enunciated in a received pronunciation BBC accent. But the pronunciation of the name of the next village, Habrough, which came out as Hahbro rather than Haybro, simply revealed the ignorance of southerners, didn't it?

On the appointed day, the whole troop turned out in neatly pressed uniform, and I, as troop leader, had been well drilled in how to salute with the flag. We waited eagerly on Pelham Road, in front of the Scouts' meeting room, next to the 'Tin Mish', trying to appear eager but nonchalant. Sometime after 6 o'clock the royal car approached, and we heard cheers to our left, growing louder as it came towards our position. When our new Skip caught a glimpse of the maroon Rolls-Royce, he gave the signal, and I gently and carefully lowered the flag, the base of its staff in the leather holster hanging from my neck and shoulder, laid the flag deferentially from left to right in anticipation of the royal presence, and tried to look serious as Her Majesty passed, smiling broadly as she always did, and regally waving her white-gloved right hand as the car drove sedately by.

It was in the Scouts that I expanded my show business experience beyond the primary school nativity play and my performances with the skiffle group. In successive autumn seasons in the late fifties, I participated, along with others from the Immingham troop, in the Grimsby and Cleethorpes Gang Show, a local version of the London show founded and directed by Ralph Reader, who had started with a similar venture before the war.

Week after week, from September until late November, my brother John and I would travel on Saturday evenings to Grimsby, often on our bikes, for rehearsals in singing and dancing along with other members of the 'gang' – Scouts from other troops in the Grimsby and Cleethorpes area. Perhaps twenty or so items would be rehearsed, each of us learning our steps and our hand and arm movements, to perform a medley of Cockney songs, an American cowboy dance routine, a girls' school hockey number (reminiscent of St. Trinian's – except that all the cast members were boys, wearing pigtail wigs), a routine to what sounded vaguely like a Chinese tune, or a Scottish dance based on a Highland Fling. There was a terrific camaraderie as we pranced around the floor of the hired school hall, and in our mid-teens many of us ogled a beautiful, high-heeled young woman of nineteen or so who sat alluringly on the stage concentrating on sewing costumes.

Eventually the big event arrived, and after school in Barton, the bus ride home and a quick meal, I caught a public bus to Grimsby and then to Cleethorpes for the Theatre Royal. The Monday night, allotted to a dress rehearsal, was always frantically exciting. We had to get all our costumes – mostly hired from the same company that had supplied the London cast – for the various items we were performing in, and for each we would have stage make-up applied by someone who was adept at these matters. More impressively, we had our legs and arms painted with what looked like cocoa mixture, so that we would not look washed-out under the stage lights, particularly under the ultra-violet light that illuminated our white 'Greek' costumes in a song called 'The Greeks Had a Word For It'.

Donning our costumes, performing our song-and-dance routine, rushing back to change into our next costume while a sketch was being performed by a smaller group from the cast, then waiting in the wings, in silent excitement, for the curtain to rise for our entrance for the next dance: this was fun! Throughout each performance, our eyes would be on Ken Hodson, the conductor and inspiration of the Grimsby gang show, a local probation officer who was made an honorary member of the Musicians' Union so that he could be allowed to conduct the professional musicians and direct the whole show from the orchestra pit. As a finale, there was always a big singing number, a medley by the full cast, ranged on several rows of benches, with arms rocking and waving and hands fluttering, ending with what was almost a Scout anthem: 'We're Riding Along On the Crest of a Wave'.

Then it was off with the face make-up, a dash for the last bus to Immingham, perhaps half an hour to complete the unfinished homework, then to bed in order to rise in time for the school bus the following morning. This routine went on for a week, with remarkably enthusiastic audiences – mainly, I suppose, consisting of friends and relations of the cast, although I did persuade our hairdresser Sid Heyhoe to purchase a ticket on at least one occasion. To the disgust of a friend who also participated in the show, I tended to keep the 'cocoa' on my legs for the whole week: it was too much trouble washing it off each night only to have it reapplied the following evening, and my mother never complained about the colour of the sheets.

I think I took part in the Gang Show for three successive years, and in one of those years, 1959, some of the Gang came to Immingham to put on a fund-raiser in recognition of our contribution to the Grimsby and Cleethorpes show. After that, I left for University, but in the autumn of 1961 I made a point of returning to join the audience for an early evening half-hour performance that was broadcast live on Children's Hour on the radio. I still have a recording of that show, on a long-playing vinyl disc, and of course playing it revives memories and thoughts of what might have been if I had any real theatrical talent. The smell of the grease-paint and the roar of the crowd (or the other way round, as some wit quipped): it was fun while it lasted, and I felt that I had experienced something of the excitement that drives theatre and other performing arts. But life had other things in store for me. I left the Scouts behind, after they had given me many valuable experiences that I was unable to gain from B.G.S., since the school was located in the 'wrong' direction to allow me to get involved.

Before the Scouts, I had enjoyed another hobby to which I devoted a great deal of energy and enthusiasm. In my boyhood, despite my father's enthusiastic trade unionism, which ought to have inclined him towards the *Daily Herald*, the newspaper of choice in the household was the *News Chronicle*, a distinguished Liberal-leaning organ in its day. This was delivered to the house each morning. In the evenings we took the *Grimsby Evening Telegraph*, and once a week the *Lincolnshire Times*. In the 1950s, the *Chronicle* launched its 'I-Spy Club' for children.

This was an elaborate enterprise based on a North American Indian motif. 'Big Chief I-Spy' was the nominal head of this 'tribe', its members 'Redskins'. It published booklets on a couple of dozen themes – birds; trees; the seaside; cars; a train journey; ships and harbours: I have forgotten most by now – each page containing a couple of line drawings of objects that related to the theme, plus a number denoting how many points each object was 'worth': the less common the object, the higher the value. Each object was also accompanied by one or two lines for the reader to state where the object was seen, and the date. The idea was that the young 'Redskin' would go around eagerly looking for items that featured in the little books, write down the date and place and proudly tot up the points – say, 10 for a thatched cottage, an oak tree or a blackbird; 15 for a thatched church, a yew or a heron; more for less common objects. When a milestone was reached – 1,000 points – the book would be duly sent off to Bouverie Street, EC4, where one imagined the entries would in some mysterious way be validated (more likely, I would now say, a 17-year-old office worker casually checked the total of points, if that), and the book would be returned with a feather dyed in some lurid colour that reflected the theme of the book. These feathers could be made into a head-dress to display one's prowess in spotting items as one went about one's daily life or travelled on holiday.

I joined in the summer of 1951, soon after my eighth birthday. On a trip to Cleethorpes, I bought my first 'I-Spy' book from 'Big Chief Eagle Eye' and I was hooked. I acquired all the little books as they came out, thereby setting myself unrealistic goals, because I could never have known what the full range of items was, let alone be aware that I had actually seen something for which I might have been awarded points leading to another feather. A better strategy would have been to specialise on a few books. It was a replica of my strategy towards poetry: aiming to memorise 'The Pied Piper of Hamelin' meant that I learned not a single poem.

On one occasion we took the train to Cleethorpes for a 'pow-wow' – a gathering of 'Redskins' and their families on the beach at low tide. We waited eagerly until 'Big Chief I-Spy' in full Indian costume, including an impressive head-dress with long tails adorned with feathers, came galloping up on a magnificent skewbald horse, swerved in an arc to a dramatic halt, raised his right hand and solemnly gave the traditional greeting: 'How!' A couple of hundred or more ardent followers responded with their own enthusiastic 'How!' On another occasion, 12 June 1954, we took a train to London for a big – in fact, a 'monster' – 'pow-wow' attended by some six thousand 'Redskins' and their families.

This was an unusual day out for us that we could afford thanks to concessionary travel for a railway worker's family. Unfortunately, our train arrived late at King's Cross, and whoever was in charge of our London Transport tour bus was a little rattled by the time we turned up on the South Bank near the Festival Hall. But off we went on a tour of the 'sights', giving an opportunity to complete the book of 'The Sights of London' and earn another feather, followed by a visit to a dress rehearsal of 'White Horse Inn on Ice' at the Empire Pool, Wembley. It was all good, clean family fun, a rare experience for us, and an occasion that boosted my enthusiasm for the 'I-Spy Club'.

My mother declared that my keen interest in 'I-Spy' made me 'observant'. I wasn't quite sure what this meant, but I assumed it was a good thing, given the tone with which she uttered the phrase to family and visiting friends. And I certainly have a tendency to notice things that others frequently miss – something that has helped me as a proof-reader and editor – but there could be any number of explanations for that. The main effect, of course, was to make sure my parents continued to buy the *News Chronicle* – and a subsidiary purpose was to make me grow up as a reader of that paper. Alas, it folded in 1960, by which time I had long lost interest in 'I-Spy', which in any case had dwindled from an active movement of perhaps hundreds of thousands to a three-inch column in the newspaper (it continued in the *Daily Mail* for a while), mentioning some object of interest for young readers to look out for.

We also tried our hand – or our eye – at another observation game promoted by the same newspaper in the 1950s: spotting the fictional character 'Lobby Lud' whenever he was in Cleethorpes (once or twice a season, I think). Each day during the summer, the paper would carry a silhouette or photograph of the trilby-hatted individual's partially obscured face – from the side, or looking from behind a newspaper, or lighting a cigarette – and indicate the seaside resort in which he would be present on that particular day: Scarborough and Filey last week, Skegness today, Mablethorpe tomorrow, then Cleethorpes. Anyone who believed they had identified him was invited to approach him carrying a copy of that day's *Chronicle*, and accurately utter the magical formula: 'You are Mr Lobby Lud and I claim my five pounds prize'. Needless to say, we never spotted him, and in any case, donkey rides, sand castles, paddling in the sea, riding on roundabouts, catching shrimps with nets in rock pools or, as we grew older, slipping pennies into slot machines or sixpenny pieces into jukeboxes engaged our attention rather than the elusive emissary of the *News Chronicle*. I felt an echo of this half a century later, though, when in O'Connell Street in Dublin's city centre I was approached by two schoolgirls, no doubt intrigued by my black raincoat and fedora, to ask whether I was the then equivalent of Lobby Lud, whose presence on the street had been announced by a local radio station. Even more startlingly, I was asked by a schoolgirl on her way home from class one day whether I

JOHN AND RONALD HILL,
CLEETHORPES BEACH, C. 1950

was Michael Jackson. She was evidently too young to know that the American singer had actually been dead for several years by then – and in any case my black fedora was not quite the style of hat that he wore on stage.

About the same time as I-Spy, I took up the hobby of train-spotting as the serious pastime that almost all schoolboys engaged in at some stage. The Ian Allan booklets, each containing lists of the numbers of every locomotive on the various divisions of British Railways – ours was the London and North Eastern Railway, the L.N.E.R. – became a constant pocket companion. The number of every engine I saw – either from the front or from the side of the driver's cab – would be carefully noted and crossed out or underlined in the appropriate book. My older cousin Brian, also a keen train-spotter, taught me the trick of reading the number of a locomotive on a passing train: stand by the window in the corridor and twist the head rapidly to the right while looking down to the appropriate height on the engine. With good eyesight, and a dose of luck, it was possible to register the number, and the happy spotter could mark off another in the book.

We boys – I don't think it was a hobby that attracted girls – learned a lot about identifying locomotives from such details as funnel height, the presence of 'blinkers' (smoke deflectors) or of streamlining, and above all the wheel configurations of various types, a standard scheme of classification: 0–4–0, 2–4–0, 4–6–0. Mumbo-jumbo to the uninitiated. Travelling by train via Doncaster to Sheffield, Leeds, York or London, say, gave opportunities to see some of the famous locomotives as they passed through at speed on their way between London and Leeds, York, Newcastle or Edinburgh. Seeing 'namers' – engines that carried a name as well as a number – was particularly gratifying. On a lucky occasion, even a famous engine such as the magnificent A4 class 4–6–2 *Mallard* – holder of the world steam speed record of 126 m.p.h., designed by Sir Nigel Gresley, with a capacity of eight tons of coal and 5,000 gallons of water (the kind of detail any train-spotter worth his salt would carry in his head) – could be spotted in its shining blue livery speeding through on its way to King's Cross. The biggest thrill for any train-spotter was to be allowed to step up briefly on to the footplate – usually in response to the query to the driver: 'Can I cab you, mister?'.

Dad sometimes gave me insight into the skills required to operate these high-speed, long-distance beasts. One of the functions of a fireman, apart from keeping the fire stoked up, was picking up water from troughs that lay between the rails of the track. Although these were several hundred yards long and contained a thousand gallons or more of water, it was crucial for the pick-up tube to be lowered at the right moment to hit the start of the trough, so as to get the maximum advantage: a tricky enough operation at speed. I think a railway water trough was worth ten or fifteen 'I-Spy' points.

Apart from these activities, there were other sources of amusement and entertainment in our household, including various animals. After our cat, Jos, had been put down following her failure to settle in Immingham, the home was not long without pets. Indeed, we usually had livestock of some kind around us. Not cattle, sheep or pigs, of course, but domestic – or domesticated – pets. Not all were ours by choice, but they demanded our attention and provided an interest and sometimes amusement.

We always kept hens, or at least Dad did, in a crudely constructed hen house at the bottom of the garden. Usually bought as fluffy yellow day-old chicks, they were kept indoors for a few days and fed meal, then transferred into their accommodation, with its wire-enclosed area in which they could scratch, peck, and dust themselves. They matured, grew feathers, and as pullets, encouraged by the introduction of a porcelain dummy egg, began to use an attached array of straw-lined laying boxes from which we would collect eggs that my father sold year-round for four shillings a dozen, regardless of the market price. He never really understood supply and demand, so that when there was a glut and the shop price fell, he would be left with unsold eggs; demand would return when his four-shillings-a-dozen eggs were cheaper than what could be obtained in the local grocer's.

Dad always had 'plans' to expand this activity, buying *The Smallholder* and scouring the advertisements. It was a hobby that he aspired to turn into a business, although he had neither the knowledge nor, I think, the temperament to make a success of it. But I'm sure it formed an essential part of our family budget. Eggs came 'free', and as often as not so did Christmas dinner. Turkey was never on the menu; a goose did once make an appearance, but normally it was one of our own chickens, selected pretty randomly, and despatched by a neighbour: Dad tried once but the bird refused to die. In Barnetby the neighbour was Mr Carline. Strong as an ox, he would hold the bird under his left arm, grasp the head in his right hand, give it a yank, twist the body a couple of times, and that was it, Dad would painstakingly pluck the feathers, and the unpleasant task of cleaning out the innards fell to my mother's more delicate hands – to the disgust of my brother and me, for whom the smell was overpowering. Airwick came into its own on these occasions.

We never replaced Jos, but we had a succession of goldfish, won as prizes at village fetes or visiting funfairs, which we kept in globe-shaped bowls and fed with ant eggs, while allowing Mam to change the water as she deemed necessary, sometimes with our help. One of these was given the unlikely name of 'Cuthbert', and he featured in one of my English class compositions in 1954, including details of his living quarters: 'a goldfish bowl, a weed and some coloured pebbles'; the latter, I wrote, 'help to keep the water clean'. On more than one occasion, as the water was being poured out, the unfortunate fish slipped into the sink, and had to be rescued, wriggling, and placed back into its bowl. I seem to remember that one little fish managed to negotiate the U-bend and end up outside the house – but perhaps that's just a 'memory' planted by a joking uncle.

We adopted a hedgehog that appeared in the garden, feeding it with milk and warming it in front of the fire, until Mam noticed the eggs of some parasite or other among the spines and the wretched animal was banished.

We also took in a sparrow with an injured leg. The poor thing couldn't fly, of course, and could move only with difficulty. John and I deemed it in need of care and attention. We gave it a name: Pip. I went on my bike to the village chemist and bought a small tin of Germolene, which I applied to the injury, and we lovingly tended the little bird, encouraging it to drink water and to eat breadcrumbs – all to no avail. Pip died within a day, and was solemnly buried in the garden beside the rhubarb. We erected a gravestone to mark the spot: a brick on which we scratched 'Here lies Pip, a sparrow', plus no doubt a cross, and the date on which we committed his (or her) soul to the Almighty.

We were rather more successful in keeping a magpie, 'Maggie', who adopted us rather than the other way round. He survived our company for ten days or so one summer, perhaps because we fed him and thereby became a reliable source of food. He would come into the house, and no doubt leave droppings in places we'd rather he didn't, but we accepted him. When my mother was serving peas one lunchtime, Maggie hopped across the table and helped himself. Even that was not too much to tolerate. But when he started strutting into neighbours' open bedroom windows on warm nights and pecking at their overnight hairpins, my parents decided that this was going too far. Since we could not confine him, or train him to act with appropriate restraint when dealing with our neighbours, he had to go. My father cadged a cardboard box from a shop, we caught Maggie, bade our fond farewells as we put him into the box, and strapped the whole thing on to the parcel carrier on my Dad's bike. Three miles away, he was returned to nature in a local wood.

The family – and the neighbours – proved rather less tolerant of our next pets: mice. My brother John and a friend, Spike, cycled to Grimsby one summer afternoon, and returned with two mice that John had bought in a pet shop, for a shilling or so apiece. Since both were entirely grey, there was nothing about their appearance to distinguish them from wild mice, but their provenance was such that they were deemed to be pets. John, aged about twelve, announced to our mother that he had bought 'one of each', and they were duly kept in separate cages in our outhouse and fed water and oats. All seemed to be going well with these unexpected – and, as far as our parents were concerned, uninvited – guests. After a few days, though, my mother, doing a bit of dusting in the front room, with the window wide open to let in air, overheard a snatch of conversation between John and his friend.

'They must be lonely,' said John.

– 'Yes,' agreed Spike.

– 'Let's put them together. Just for a few minutes.'
Mam knew precisely what they were talking about.

– 'DON'T YOU DARE!' she yelled.
It was too late. The two animals were returned to their separate cages, but three weeks later we discovered a nest with a litter of tiny pink mouselets, with snouts like little pigs, beside adult mice that looked threateningly large in comparison, and would no doubt have used their sharp incisors on our fingers had we attempted to separate them from their offspring. The little ones developed rapidly, grew fur, and had a knack of climbing up the walls of their wooden box and escaping through the wire mesh that was supposed to contain them. A few weeks later neighbours noticed mice in their outhouses. They were not pleased, but they gallantly declared that the little creatures were not our responsibility – yet my suspicions have always remained.

Rabbits came next: less threatening, obviously, than mice, and more cuddly. My brother and I had a succession of these animals, all females, kept in individual cages that it was our responsibility to clean out – a Saturday morning chore that was as often overlooked as completed. We were anxious to produce baby rabbits, partly with the aim of selling them for pocket money to unsuspecting friends. I borrowed the services of a silver-grey male owned by a school mate, and satisfied my adolescent curiosity by watching as the act of mating was accomplished. If we had reached genetics in our biology lessons we could have understood the miracle of breeding as offspring of different colours emerged, according to the proportions identified by Mendel through his observation of peas. What we did learn is that at thirty days or so, the parents really wanted nothing more to do with their progeny: they attacked them and chased them away, so my brother and I had to find new homes for them. Many parents half a century later wish they could be as heartless to their offspring, for whom home comforts trump independent living.

For several years we also had a tortoise, named Tim. Not much emotional response from him, but we took our responsibilities for his welfare quite seriously. Unlike some of our neighbours, we did not drill a hole in his shell and tether him: that seemed unnecessarily cruel. Instead, we tried to contain him within a chicken-wire fenced enclosure that enabled him to wander in a restricted area in search of food and shade, and I'm sure we gave him a saucer of water, which we topped up when we remembered. Occasionally he would force his way beneath the fence and plod off into the vegetable plot. Slowly but determinedly, and with malice aforethought, he headed in the direction of fresh heads of crisp lettuce. He survived several winters, cocooned in hay or straw inside a cubic wooden box in the outhouse from where the mice had long escaped. One winter he woke during an unexpected January warm spell, yawned (well, so it appeared) and nibbled at some food placed in front of his mouth, then returned to his hibernation and slept until spring arrived. His repeated survival puzzled me. He ate, so far as I could judge, little more than lettuce leaves – and he certainly consumed significant quantities of those, to my father's annoyance. But lettuce leaves, consisting of water and not much else, are for slimmers. How a cold-blooded creature can survive on an anorexic diet, let alone build up stores of fat to get it through the winter, is one of the profound mysteries of Nature beyond my understanding. One year, he failed to make it through, and was duly buried deep in our back garden, but without the reverence accorded to Pip the sparrow.

One thing I learned from my association with this inconstant menagerie was that animals tie you down. Some can be fed every two or three days, but most need daily attention. The hens required food, water and grit, any eggs had to be collected from the nesting boxes, and the coop should ideally be fastened at night against predators. Going away for a few days, let alone on a family holiday, required that arrangements for their care be put in place. Lengthy holidays were a rarity in our family, but occasionally a neighbour would have to be engaged to keep an eye on things while we were away visiting relatives for a weekend, or on the occasional longer trip. Still, I'm sure we learned a lot from being owners of sentient beings that relied on us for their welfare. I would hardly call the experience *fun* – I suspect that requires a dog or a horse – but it was part of our development, and it offered distraction of a kind that the modern pursuit of games on screens cannot.

A final interest that I developed while I was still in Barnetby primary school, and that in a sense has stayed with me throughout my life, was friendship with other children around the world. In May 1951, quite out of the blue, a letter arrived with an unusual stamp, addressed to me. Letters for eight-year-olds were rare occurrences, let alone letters from exotic locations. This one came from the Gold Coast, about which I knew absolutely nothing. Following the royal footsteps of King George V, I had been collecting stamps for a couple of years by then, and this unusual addition enhanced my collection, along with others that I could not identify, given the unfamiliar alphabet: they came from Bulgaria and Serbia, as I later discovered.

Stamp collecting first introduced me to a phenomenon that has mushroomed in recent years with the rapid rise of the Internet: mail order shopping. Periodically I would go to the post office to buy a postal order to send to Stanley Gibbons, the world-famous stamp dealers, in response to advertisements in the *Eagle* weekly comic, and a week or ten days later the post office would deliver my order of a package of selected stamps, or stamp hinges for mounting them in my album, or tweezers for handling the stamps without damage from my sweaty and grubby fingers. Or in secondary school, when I was already taking lessons in chemistry, I would order test tubes or simple chemicals to replenish or extend the stock in a chemistry set that I had received as a Christmas or birthday present.

I once sent off a two-shilling postal order to some company or other, probably in a warehouse in East London, and received a 'Seebackroscope' – a novelty item that I found distinctly disappointing. A plastic eye-piece fitted into the socket of the right eye, rather like a monocle; this narrowed to a closed tube with a 45-degree end, on the inside of which was a mirror; the outer side of the tube contained an oval hole through which an image of an object somewhere over one's shoulder would enter, reflect on the mirror and hit the retina. Alas, unlike a periscope, which really does allow a submarine crew to look above the waves in all directions, the field of vision of the 'Seebackroscope' was so limited that I determined it to have been a foolish waste of my pocket money, and I resolved not to be taken in again. I am, perhaps for that reason, a reluctant user of eBay.

In response to my unexpected letter from foreign parts, the atlas revealed the Gold Coast to be a small country on the coast of West Africa, then a British colony, and the letter came from a schoolboy whose nickname – 'Yankee Boy' – and address I have retained in my mind:

Catholic Senior School,
Kuntanasi,
Via Kumasi,
Ashanti,
Gold Coast.

I never found out how he obtained my name and address: hardly through St. Barnabas' Church of England primary school, since his school was run by Catholics, although it may conceivably have been passed on through *Good Housekeeping* magazine, which had my address from the competition that I had entered with my rhyme on 'Roses are red'. I didn't ponder for too long. This was a very exciting event in my life, and I engaged in an exchange of letters that continued after we moved to Immingham at the end of the year.

Some months after that move, I received another unusual piece of mail: a package from 'Yankee Boy' that turned out to contain a monkey skin, which I ecstatically took to school to show Miss Summers and the class. It was essentially parchment, although to me it was rather like thick brown paper, with longish black hair on one side. I sensed that this was something rather special among the people of the Gold Coast, but I am still not sure what I was expected to do with it: hang it on a wall, perhaps. In the event, it was put away and when I rediscovered it after a year or so moth larvae had done their worst. I lost contact with 'Yankee Boy' – I suspect he was several years older than me; I still have his photo – but I have retained a fond although unprofessional interest in the country that became Ghana in 1957.

In my first or second year in B.G.S. I started corresponding with a boy in the Hungarian capital, Budapest. His name was Biró Csaba, which of course I could not correctly pronounce – and neither did I then know that in Hungarian the surname precedes the given name. We corresponded for two or three years, exchanging letters and photographs, and I received a holiday postcard from him in Transylvania, which years later I discovered is a Hungarian-populated region of modern Romania that had been part of Hungary until the First World War. I was alarmed when I heard of the Soviet invasion of Hungary in the autumn of 1956, and saw photographs of Soviet tanks in the streets of Budapest and then columns of wretched Hungarian families heading towards the border with Austria. After a few weeks I received a letter, in halting English, obviously composed with recourse to a dictionary, in which my penfriend recounted what he had experienced.

> I think you know what days lived the Hungarian people. We rebelled against the tyranny. Many young boys fought together with the grown-ups. Once I was in the street with my friends when fired at us with machine-guns. We bowed down, so lucky we are safe. Our fine capital today is very ugly. The tanks fired to the

> houses, and many houses falled down. We build barricades. The Great-Boulevard is the ugliest. There is the Kilian-barrack; that was the centre of the insurgents. In the last weeks Budapest looked terrible; on the roads there were corpses, burned out tanks, and armoured cars. Our school got many fire. The step was breaked down, many classrooms had great holes. I think, we have very long recess.

And he concluded:

> We are thankfull the English people wich helped us.

My friend was, sadly, misinformed, since the West did nothing to support the uprising, apart from offering bluster and propaganda. I later learned that his family had fled to France, and I lost contact with him. But when years later I became a specialist on the Soviet Union and its empire, and visited the city of Budapest, my correspondence with Csaba gave added piquancy to my study. And whenever I included excerpts from that letter in lectures to students, the words were always heard in reverential silence.

I had other penfriends, too. A German boy with a Polish surname: Kurt Ruskowski, with whom I struggled to correspond in German in response to his excellent English. A German girl, Elfriede. A French boy, Michel. A French girl as well, whose name I have long forgotten. We corresponded intermittently over a few months or a couple of years before the letters petered out. But these distant friendships had a profound long-term effect on my outlook. I developed a fascination with the outside world, with other countries and cultures, that inspired my career as a professional student of the Soviet Union, and I became a convinced internationalist.

This view of the world was enhanced when I began to learn languages other than English, starting with French under Billo at B.G.S., continuing with Latin, then teaching myself some German, studying Russian at Leeds University (and acquiring a Russian penfriend whom I met on several occasions in the Soviet Union), picking up a bit of Romanian when living as a graduate student for a year in what is now Moldova, taking Polish lessons in Warsaw and subsequently Cracow, a few Dutch lessons in the Netherlands, and dabbling in other languages via the BBC Network Three in the 1960s – some Spanish, a little Italian, and even a few words of Chinese – sufficient for me to say to a Chinese student that I am English (and for him to understand what I was saying, which was more important). A few words in an exotic or 'unusual' language go a long way with native speakers. This, too, has been a great source of satisfaction, entertainment and amusement, a hobby alongside music, theatre, literature and other arts that have come into my life since leaving my origins in North Lincs.

8

The World of Work

The performances of the Black Diamonds at local village halls, including the 'Tin Mish' in Immingham, and the Women's Institute hall at the other end of the village (also used on occasion for whist drives, beetle drives, talent shows, fêtes and other fund-raising efforts), were an occasional source of income to supplement my modest pocket money. But ten shillings, a pound, or even thirty shillings shared among several Black Diamonds did not make any of us flush with cash.

There were few opportunities for earning additional pocket money. My parents continued to give John and me a weekly allowance, which increased steadily, but not to a great extent, over the years. Dad's share was for 'saving' – for holidays, for presents, or to purchase larger items – and Mam's could be spent on the day we received it, if we so chose (it all came ultimately from Dad's wages, of course, but there was a principle that we were being taught). In my teens, the Scouts took a fair amount of my regular allowance, plus bits and pieces for my bike, the occasional ice cream or chocolate bar, perhaps a bus ride to Grimsby to look in shop windows. I never received more than five shillings a week as 'spending money' until my last few weeks at the grammar school, after I reached the age of eighteen, when my mother started giving me seven shillings and sixpence – half as much again. I knew that some of my classmates received substantially more than this, but I understood our family's circumstances and made little of it. The odd few bob from the Black Diamonds helped – but hardly transformed the situation. And, whereas children in towns had a variety of opportunities for a weekly job – in a shop on Saturdays, for example, or doing a paper delivery round – an industrial village offered very little, and the fact that I attended school a forty-minute bus ride away ruled out a morning job.

More effective in giving a brief boost was the autumn potato-picking season. In those days, Lincolnshire was still a major area for growing the staple vegetable of British, Irish, and in general Northern European cuisine: the spud. Hundreds of acres of land that is now given over to oil-seed rape were devoted to its cultivation, and from late September or early October onwards casual work was available for teams of unskilled labourers. A regular supply of workers came from across the Irish Sea. Teams, or gangs, of workers from Sligo, Leitrim, Roscommon or Mayo, desperate for work and income to support their families in a decade when Ireland suffered severe poverty and deprivation, would travel from farm to farm offering their services. The post offices did a roaring trade in postal orders as these workers remitted part of their earnings to their wives and families on the Emerald Isle. They would be joined by gangs of local workers, often housewives looking for pin money in the weeks before Christmas, who were picked up by special buses from assembly points and delivered to the fields of individual farmers. My mother joined such teams for several years, and on two or three occasions so did my brother and I, during the autumn half-term holiday and at weekends before and after this break in the school routine.

The work was physically demanding, but required no intellect. It is now done by machine. In those days, a tractor would drag a piece of equipment to turn the soil and lift out the tuber-laden potato plants. The workers would move in, pick up the potatoes and put them into wicker baskets ('skips'), which they would tip into an open trailer pulled by a tractor that followed the first. Sometimes, depending on how heavy the crop was and the speed of the first tractor, there would be an opportunity to rest briefly until the next stint; but it was still a tiring day's work for a teenager used to a sedentary life sitting at a school desk. The money – perhaps two or three pounds, or even a fiver, for the week – made it worthwhile, and I squandered some of it on trying to demonstrate how grown-up I was: I bought a packet of ten cigarettes, with which I showed off by puffing at the back of the school bus. Mercifully, I never became hooked on the weed: I had more lasting things to spend my money on, it ran out, and in any case I never persevered with smoking beyond the sense of feeling sick every time I inhaled.

One year, I think before the potato picking, I did a stint for my Uncle Charlie, who had a small farm at Keelby, a few miles from home. A mere thirty acres or so, it had a few cattle and hens, plus fields for tillage, so it was not lavishly equipped: nothing much beyond a tractor and a trailer or two, a plough, a couple of harrows, a drilling machine for sowing the grain seed, and perhaps a mower to cut grass for hay and the wheat for threshing. It was perhaps typical of many family farms in those years before combine harvesters came to dominate grain production and massive bales of hay and straw, wrapped in black plastic, dominated the landscape after the harvest. A large piece of equipment such as a threshing machine, for separating the grain from the ears of wheat or barley, would travel from one small farm to another on a contract basis, hired for a week or so at a time. The same went for static baling machines to process the straw after threshing. My job, which lasted a week or so, consisted in threading iron wire into the baler. Straw from the thresher was fed into one end; the baler compressed it and forced it through a square-section chamber, and at a certain point three feet or so of compressed straw was tied off by the machine, which twisted together the two wires, and the bales were slowly edged off the machine for stacking by farm workers stronger than I was at that stage. The bales were quite heavy, and the wires could damage hands if not handled with a degree of acquired skill.

Within a few years, in my later teens, the technology had moved on, when I found several weeks' work on one rather larger local farm in Immingham, the Beacocks'. The family were stalwarts of the Methodist chapel to which my brother and I were sent on Sunday mornings, and at which the head of the house, Mr Beacock, was a lay preacher. He was by that stage elderly, bald, sun-tanned beneath the line of his flat cap, and his back severely bent from being required, at the age of sixteen, to lift heavy sacks of grain. His elder son, Ralph, with his wife ran a greengrocer's and florist's shop in the village, and his younger son, Eric, was a pupil in Barton Grammar School a couple of years ahead of me. I was familiar with the farm and was delighted to have a chance to work during the summer holiday, when the whole Beacock family pitched in with the harvest and additional hands were hired as well.

It was approaching the end of an era, when farming techniques that had been in use for several generations – since the start of mechanisation – were being replaced by more modern, capital-intensive methods. The

Beacocks did hire an early combine harvester to get in part of their crop, and after that machine had gone over a field, all that remained was to bale the straw, using a moveable, tractor-drawn machine, which picked up the cut straw, compressed it and tied it off with twine into bales. A tractor followed later pulling a blue-painted sledge comprising an iron frame with a base of steel slats; bales would be stacked on to this contraption, and when a pile of suitable height had been made, a lever would release the hinged back of the frame, and friction with the stubble beneath would leave the neat pile of bales to be collected by a tractor and trailer for leading back to the farm for storage in a barn.

This was cutting-edge technology in the late 1950s, and the traditional methods, in use for well over a century, also persisted. The ripened wheat or barley would be cut by a tractor-drawn mower, tied with twine into bundles known as sheaves, and left to lie on the cut stubble. The job of the field hands was to lift these sheaves and stack eight or ten of them, seed end up towards the sun, in the form of a stook (pronounced stowk in the local dialect), nudging the ears so that the one sheaf would intertwine with and support its neighbours. The whole process was known as 'stowking'. There was a knack to it, particularly in getting the first two sheaves to stand without support from the next pair; and the constant bending, lifting and carrying was pretty tiring until one grew used to it. In handling the cut corn, barley was by far the most difficult. Although it was lighter to lift and carry than wheat, the brittle spikes or awns on the ears of seed are much longer, and they would easily break and pieces work their way under clothing, lodging in folds in the skin, and irritating us workers. The modern combine harvester eliminates that.

A couple of weeks or so later, provided there had been sun to ripen the ears, the stooks would be dismantled as the sheaves were transferred by cart to the corner of the field and made into a stack (also known as a rick) that would stand until January, the slack season for field work, when threshing would take place. This was a somewhat more skilled task: creating both a cartload and a stack that would be stable enough to withstand movement and the winter elements, and also be constructed in such a way as to keep the precious grains dry. A novice could easily build a stack in a lopsided way, and the higher the build the less stable it became, so the corners and outside edges were left to experienced farmers. Using a two-pronged pitchfork, I was initially allowed to pass the sheaves from the cart to the individuals who were building the stack, and when I gained some experience, to work on the inside of the stack, picking up and laying the individual sheaves.

The knack lay in 'stabbing' the individual sheaf in precisely the right position with the pitchfork so that it would be well balanced and not fall off, and also would allow the easy removal of the fork, without getting tangled in the twine binding. The ideal position was to strike with the fork into the sheaf just below the binding, to balance the head of grain. The fork could then be easily manoeuvred using both hands and arms, lifting the sheaf – passing it down from the cart at the start of the stack, and increasingly upward and over-arm as the building of the stack progressed to twenty feet or more. Again, this activity was quite strenuous to someone not used to manual labour, and I would end up with aching arms, shoulders, back, thighs and lower legs from bracing and lifting scores if not hundreds of sheaves in the course of a daily shift. More than once I misjudged my aim with the pitchfork, which would become entangled with the binder twine, and the sheaf would not disengage when I lifted it. The old worker on the top of the stack would struggle to release the sheaf, and on one occasion, with a broad smile, enquired in a smattering of Lincolnshire dialect that had all but died out: 'Ar nailt 'er?' (Have you nailed it?).

The work was exhilarating, if tiring, but not well paid. It brought in some pocket money, it kept me out of the house, it gave me exercise, and at least it meant I could look my Dad in the eye and say I really was working.

It is a long time since I lost contact with farming: I wonder how many of these techniques, and the items of equipment that were used to accomplish them, are still in existence – or are even remembered by farmers of today. Very few, I suspect.

At the age of fourteen, I did find a Saturday morning job that helped boost my finances significantly – or, rather, my mother found it for me. Cook's bakery, at the north end of the village, supplied bread, rolls, cakes and confectionery through the family shop in the centre of Immingham, opposite the County Hotel, and also to local villages: Keelby, Brocklesby, Great Limber and elsewhere within a ten-mile radius. Old Mr Cook, approaching retirement age, intimated that he would welcome an assistant, and I was duly taken on. Each Saturday morning, I would turn up at the shop, where Mr Cook would already have loaded his blue

Commer van with wooden trays of his wares, and we would set off on a delivery route that would take two or three hours.

It was a regular circuit, and no doubt Mr Cook had been following it for years, two or three times a week. He knew his customers and their buying habits. We would arrive at a particular house and stop. At the back of the van, Mr Cook would place in a large wicker basket a selection of the products that he felt the lady of the house might be interested in. An unsliced white loaf, plus perhaps half a dozen bridge rolls and a sponge cake here; a wholemeal, a crusty cob and some jam tarts or a Swiss roll there; a sliced Nimble loaf and possibly a pack of crumpets at a third. And he might add the weekly bill for payment. Usually he got the selection right, and I would take the money with the empty basket back to the van; sometimes there would be a request for something special – perhaps for a birthday celebration – and I would return to the van to supplement my stock. It was a pleasant enough way to spend a Saturday morning – getting to know some of the villages in the area, meeting people, and feeling that I was doing something useful. On a bitterly cold morning, when my hands were blue with the chill, Mr Cook turned to me: 'Sit on them!,' he instructed. It worked, and I have always remembered that little trick derived from experience of life.

I was never given any pay for my efforts. To keep it more or less legal, ten shillings was handed to my mother on the following Monday. 'If anybody asks you,' said Mr Cook, 'I don't pay you.' I understood that this was technically correct – and how my ten shillings a week went through his accounts was something I never discovered or enquired about.

Another more or less reliable source of pocket money was a job working on the Christmas post, but there weren't many such jobs in the small post office in Immingham. I did manage to get one for a couple of years, after disappointment the first time I applied. For most of the time, I worked in the sorting office, slotting envelopes into boxes for the individual streets in the village, making piles in numerical order, separately odd and even since the 'Postie' delivered to one side of the street and then the other, and tying them with rough string, using a slip knot. Postal workers were perfectly adept at tying this, but I needed several attempts to discover the secret. Slotting the letters into the individual sorting boxes on the wall in front of me, too, was an acquired skill: slow at first, until the layout of the boxes for the various streets became familiar, but then much speedier, and since it was not particularly arduous or mentally demanding, I could enjoy banter with other temporary workers, and with the permanent staff who knew the delivery rounds, and could put together bundles in the appropriate order.

On some days, I would accompany a worker on her round, riding a Post Office bicycle, straining my back by lugging a heavy sack of bundles of letters, caring for my fingers by approaching spring-loaded letter boxes with caution, and trying to avoid the canines and incisors of the occasional fierce dog – for which the advice of the regular Postie was invaluable. It was all good fun, and one learned a little about how postal workers went about their week in, week out task that we all take for granted. This was about the time Christmas Day deliveries ceased – much to the relief of the female postal workers, whose Christmas dinner preparations had been delayed. In subsequent years, after my family moved to Scunthorpe, I worked in the parcel despatch office – putting parcels into sacks for individual counties for delivery to the railway station at the start of their onward journey to all parts of the country and the world. Except that not every county had its sack: 'Lincs and Hunts' covered Huntingdonshire and part of Lincolnshire, for example, and I cannot imagine that Rutland had its separate sack – England's famously smallest county, as everyone knew, abolished (to be later revived) in the reform of local government, when Lindsey also disappeared into 'Humberside'.

Another summer my brother John and I found temporary employment in a frozen food factory in Grimsby, where for the first time I experienced the regulated life of a factory worker. The idea of a shift of a specific length, and of using a time clock to start and finish work, of being in a hierarchy of authority, power and responsibility, was new to me after years in school that were regulated by the clock, certainly, but were regarded as only part of one's occupation. With study as a way of life, there is never an ending: one cannot stop thinking, and so, even away from the environment of an educational establishment, the process of 'work' continues. In most jobs, by contrast, one works in a specific place for a certain number of hours; outside those hours, one is not working. It's part of the definition, and it took some getting used to.

Staying in what had been our grandmother's house in Clayton Street, Grimsby, by then owned by our Auntie Jean, we would cycle through the early-morning streets to clock in for work a few minutes before 6 or 7.30 a.m. or 2.p.m, for an eight-hour shift. My job was on a processing line handling peas. They would arrive at the factory by the lorry-load, direct from the viners that removed them from their shells, sometimes as far away as Kent, several hours' drive away. After blanching in boiling water, followed by cooling, they would move on a conveyor belt at which white-turbaned women would stand to pick out discoloured peas. Apparently pigeons can be trained to perform this task, which must have been dizzying and tiring on the eyes of these women: millions of peas would pass before them in an hour. The blanched peas would then be lifted overhead and fed via a hopper into the machine that I was operating, alongside several other processing lines. I was dressed, for reasons of hygiene, in white overalls and rubber boots, with a white cap to keep my hair in check as I worked, sometimes at a quite frantic pace.

A vertical cylinder, ten inches or a foot across, would automatically fill from the hopper, and the peas would fall immediately on to an aluminium tray of perhaps two feet by three. I then moved the charged tray along an array of rollers, picked up and placed the next tray, swung the double-headed cylinder clockwise to release another tray-load, slid it left behind the previous tray, placed another tray in its place, swung the cylinder unit anti-clockwise to release a further tray-load, and so on. Swing, slide, place next tray; swing, slide, place next tray; swing, slide ... Another operative at the end of the line would pick up the charged trays and slide them into the racks of a stacking trolley, and with its full load of trays this would be wheeled into the freezing room by workers equipped with Arctic clothing: wadded jackets and trousers, thick mittens and protective headgear.

For much of the time, the pace would be steady: a dozen or fifteen trays a minute, perhaps up to twenty. In a slack period, we could take it easy and listen to the pop music that was blaring from loudspeakers to keep the workers contented. But when a big load came in – two or three lorries from different parts of the country, perhaps, one delayed by traffic on the way – the peas might flow faster than we could operate the machine. Back-ups occurred, and sometimes peas would come spilling over the top of the hopper on to the floor. These could not, of course, be wasted. The floor was constantly being washed, so these peas would simply be shovelled on to the trays and sent for freezing along with the rest. I have heard similar tales about biscuit factories, where the product would be swept from the floor and fed into the packaging process; at least peas would be frozen and then boiled before eating. We also occasionally processed broad beans, and the pace was not quite so frantic. At other times of the year, carrots, green beans, Brussels sprouts, cauliflower and other vegetables would no doubt flow along the same processing line, and in late spring or early summer strawberries, raspberries and other fruit.

I'm sure the technology has been refined somewhat since the summer of 1961, and certainly the range of frozen food has expanded enormously. But, in common with very many who have worked in the food-processing industry, I gained both an understanding of what goes on in the life of a factory worker, and a measure of anxiety about what happens to the food before it reaches my dinner table. I enjoyed the money that I earned ready for going to university in the autumn, but I also felt relieved that, unlike some of my former school mates, I would not be consigned to such a mindless way of earning a living.

That sense was reinforced when I read some of the northern 'domestic' novels of John Braine, Alan Sillitoe and other Angry Young Men. It also informed my appreciation of Richard Hoggart's *The Uses of Literacy*, a passionate argument that I found inspiring when I read it as an undergraduate: the working-class life that it depicted rang many bells, and I think reading it was a formative experience for me.

Altogether more serious than the mindless toil of the frozen pea line was a single summer's employment in one of the steelworks in Scunthorpe. In mid-summer, the works closed down for 'stop fortnight' – a period of approximately two weeks in which the plant was thoroughly overhauled. I was assigned to a job as a fitter's mate, during which I learned something of the role of a 'mate', more famously identified with plumbers. The 'mate' was, by definition, not fully qualified; he was essentially a drudge, but meant to be learning on the job. The plumber – or fitter – could never know in advance what was needed in order repair an appliance or piece of equipment. Would an adjustment of a nut with a spanner solve the problem? Would welding be required? Was there a loose screw or a missing bolt? Did a panel need replacing? Would the appliance of lubrication release a seized-up hinge or valve? Only after examining the situation on the spot and making a diagnosis could the fitter identify which specialist tools, materials or other equipment was needed. Only then could the mate be despatched to pick up the appropriate tools, solder, lubricant or whatever from the stores.

I was a complete novice in the technology of steelworks, although from my school chemistry lessons I had learnt something about the removal of oxygen from iron ore in the smelting process, the re-injection of oxygen to convert iron into steel, and the addition of chromium to make stainless steel or other elements to make other special steels. I knew the theory of the functioning of blast furnaces, had studied the 'open hearth' method of making steel, and had learnt how the Bessemer converter worked. But what a real steelworks looked like was quite a different matter. Apart from pictures of iron ingots, and the impressive coloured photographs of long red-hot bars of steel being stretched in the rolling-mills, this was all quite new to me.

I had seen the red glow in the sky when blast furnaces were being topped up with fresh coke or ore or recycled metal. But the sight of an enormous Linz-Donawitz furnace, in which steel was made by bubbling oxygen through molten iron and then decanted into a great ladle: this was to me a wonder to behold. The scale of everything was humbling, added to the noise, the grease and the darkness, punctuated by the white heat of molten metal, the dazzling sparkle of welding arcs, the persistent smell of coke and metal that pervaded the air. A newcomer like me, unused to working in such an environment, felt vulnerable. The protective overalls – old, discarded, but more or less serviceable British Railways gear borrowed from my Dad – offered little comfort if something should go wrong.

But I would get up early in the morning, head out on my bike to the works at 5.30 to arrive in time to clock in for the six o'clock shift, and trudge to the fitters' den (whether it was called that I don't know, but that's what it felt like), where I would meet my immediate superior, a droll, bespectacled man of about thirty who had spent the best part of a decade travelling the world in the merchant marine. He came across as the ultimate cynic, aware in ways that management probably was not that a fitter could not always claim to have repaired a piece of equipment, so he struggled to dissemble.

'You go out on a job,' he said, 'and you use a spanner to change a valve setting or release an over-tight bolt. What do you put in your log? You can put "repaired so-and-so" – but you don't know that what you've done has actually solved the problem. You'll be called in and yelled at if you report doing the same job three times.'

'Ah, that's easy,' I offered. 'You don't say "repaired". What you say is "adjusted".'

I think he saw the value of such a term: technically accurate, seemingly professional, but inconclusive – so it would always get him off the hook if his mechanical intervention didn't work first time. Job done!

The demands on a fitter were intermittent: usually things went smoothly, and the work of stripping down the plant, cleaning and reassembling it all, with replacement parts and fittings as needed, was supervised by a team brought in from Austria, where the plant was designed. Occasionally, I was able to make use of my basic German to help the communication. But there was a lot of waiting around for a call to action, whereupon I would accompany 'my' fitter to the appropriate section of the plant to inspect a problem, then I might be sent to the stores – often for something as simple as a can of Plus-Gas lubricator – and return to pass the tools to the 'boss'. Halfway through the eight-hour shift we would have a break for our sandwiches and tea, and then continue until it was time to clean up before clocking off and cycling home, liberated until the following morning.

The work was not particularly strenuous, it brought in some needed income, and, like the work on the farm, in the post office, or in the frozen food factory, it gave me a chance to experience something of the working-class existence, against which I measure my subsequent career as a student, a doctoral candidate, and a university lecturer and professor. I learned to respect the lives of the millions who perform these essentially menial but important tasks, for the most part without complaint, doing the bidding of bosses who are in many cases no brighter than they are, but who have drawn a lucky card in life's lottery. At their most competent, they are true professionals, who deserve acknowledgement.

I once gained a similar experience on the railways with which I had grown up. I was home from Leeds University for part of a summer vacation, and Dad wondered whether I was interested in going on a short trip with him in his cab. This was, of course, not exactly legal, but his foreman was on holiday that week, so we decided to take the risk. I donned a set of old overalls, borrowed a shiny railwayman's cap, and accompanied Dad on my bike to the Scunthorpe depot. He clocked in, picked up his instructions and the starter for his diesel locomotive – a Brush Type 4 – and we picked our way over the tracks and climbed into the cab. Dad sat in the driver's seat to the left, his heavy-booted right foot on the Dead Man's Pedal (a safety feature in case the driver should fall ill at the controls), and I took the mate's seat, barely visible from outside through the laminated and tinted windscreen. It was all far more comfortable and clean than the footplate of steam locomotives on which Dad had served for a quarter of a century – but switching to diesel traction had demanded weeks of study in his 'free' time at home after work, followed by a trip to Ilford, in Essex, for practical training and driving experience on the track.

We had a light load of empty wagons that we were taking to Barnetby for re-routing – not a long trip, but there were a few gradients that had to be negotiated and a major junction as the three routes merged before Barnetby station. As an established driver on that route, Dad knew every gradient, every junction, every signal by heart, so the trip was entirely routine, and for someone of his experience not particularly demanding. An engine driver cannot do other than instructed by the signalman, who completes the track ahead by aligning points and then sets the signal to give permission to enter the section. In Britain, passenger trains are given priority, so a freight or goods train can be held up for lengthy periods.

We managed to get out of the yard and on to the main line, where we built up a bit of speed – reaching 35 or 40 miles an hour. It was quite exhilarating – but disconcerting to see how uneven the track is. The ride feels very smooth, but the rails are anything but true, stretching ahead in a pair of silver parallel ribbons. The modern engine, its windscreen stretching across the front, gives the driver a view that was impossible in most steam locomotives, with the firebox, boiler and chimney stretching in front of the driver's cab.

It is very easy to imagine the excitement of hurtling along in a mainline express at 90 or more miles an hour. But even at the modest pace of a goods train of empties, you are aware of the momentum. A train, with little friction between steel wheel and iron rail, cannot be stopped on a sixpence. Even without a bit of rain, or leaves on the track (a notion that provokes such merriment among journalists every autumn), to make the track slippery, a driver needs to have his wits about him: watching for signals, being aware of sections of track under repair or in need of maintenance (this appears in the driver's weekly briefing bulletin), keeping an eye open for the unexpected, not flinching when a bird comes dangerously close to the front screen. And, as Dad observed while we glided along a straight half-mile of track, coursing down a slight incline: 'If anybody steps out in front of you, there's nothing you can do.' He did once come across a body beside the line, somewhere between Scunthorpe and Doncaster, when he was on the coal run between Mexborough or Wath-upon-Dearne and the steelworks, and he was upset for a week or more. The thought reminded me of Tolstoy's novel *Anna Karenina*, which I had studied in the course of the previous academic year, and I chilled at the idea that Dad might have a distressed member of the public step in front of a train that he was driving.

His job, which he conscientiously carried out for forty-four years, from engine cleaner to fireman, then from 1952 driver of steam and eventually diesel, occasionally had its lighter moments. Once, when he was based at Immingham, he was given the task of driving a long-distance passenger train from Grimsby Town station to the terminus at Cleethorpes – three stops down the line, a matter of three miles at most. Nothing to it. So he was slightly amused when a middle-aged lady passenger, in fox fur and hat, paused beside the cab of the steam locomotive and said, 'Thank you for getting us here safely, driver.' He could hardly confess his modest contribution to the journey.

Since Dad spent most of his working life as a railwayman, and never owned a car, the train was our normal form of travel beyond the local area (where we would walk, or use a bike, or take a bus into Grimsby). Mam hopefully expressed a belief that she might be capable of handling a Mini, but for Dad there seemed no point, even though the house in Scunthorpe came with a garage and a driveway. From Immingham, a three-mile cycle to Habrough, where we paid threepence or so a day to leave our bikes in an outhouse at the Station Inn, gave us access to the whole network of British Railways. Day trips to relations in Scunthorpe and Lincoln, or to visit 'Auntie Sanders' in Sheffield, or to enjoy a day at the seaside at Cleethorpes or Scarborough, were a substitute for real family holidays, apart from the two occasions that I depicted earlier: Llandudno in September 1955 and Pevensey four years later.

Apart from a shortage of money, and perhaps an unwillingness to spend it on frivolities such as holidays, I believe my father felt acutely awkward staying away from home in hotels or guesthouses. The idea of being waited on seemed unnatural, and self-service just about allowed him to feel comfortable. His palate was unrefined, and he was unwilling to extend his range of tastes, so I grew up with practically no experience of dining out or of eating anything out of the ordinary – indeed, the very ordinary. True, the opportunities for 'exotic' food such as Italian, Chinese or Indian – not to mention Thai, Japanese, Lebanese, Mexican or all the other varieties of cuisine that have become ubiquitous in modern Britain – were pretty limited in North Lincs in the 1950s. Even so, in common with probably the bulk of the English working class, Dad's preference was for bland, plain food, and strong tea. If it was available, he always chose apple pie for dessert, with custard rather than cream. My mother was potentially more adventurous, but Dad's preference for the familiar and safe, combined with Mam's general dislike of cooking (although she produced excellent pastry), meant that the whole family had an uninteresting diet, prepared and eaten at home unless that was completely impossible. As for a dinner suit – I bought one of those when I absolutely needed one, long after I had left home. It has been a revelation to have enjoyed a career that has opened my mind (and my mouth) to cuisine that Dad would have found impossible to stomach. I except sago, tapioca and the like from that generalisation.

Dad, I need to remind myself, grew up in a very poor family. Even in his latter years, his preferred breakfast was bread and dripping from the roast pan, or failing that corn flakes. For more than four decades he would take sandwiches to work (his 'snap', as the railway worker called his packed meal – not 'lunch', given the unpredictable shift hours). On steam locomotives, his enamel water can, with a lid designed to serve as a drinking cup, would be stood on a shovel and thrust into the firebox until the water boiled to make tea. That level of culinary sophistication hardly encourages subtlety in a worker's dining repertoire.

Dad was devoted to his occupation on the railway, despite the shift work that allowed him no possibility of regular commitments to hobbies or other interests, and its steadily declining status, as government policy favoured roads and cars in the post-war period. He rarely missed a day's work – certainly not unless he was genuinely ill – and was hardly ever late. His succession of second-hand bikes, cannibalising one to keep its replacement on the road, got him to the depot in fifteen minutes and home again at the end of his shift, at whatever hour of the day or night that might be. He was meticulous about bicycle lights, keeping stocks of batteries and spare bulbs to maintain visibility. At work, he grew disillusioned as the years passed, particularly as manpower was steadily reduced by British Rail management. In 1982, he retired, a few years ahead of his official retirement date, in the hope that he might save the job of a younger worker. To my surprise, given his steadfast commitment, he didn't look back: indeed, he took on a new lease of life. He threw himself into the work of the Methodist Chapel, of which he was nominated a trustee, and took on the voluntary task of hospital visitor, attached to the chaplaincy – essentially assistant to the chaplain. And, as Elsie's health deteriorated, he assumed the burden of shopping and of caring for her, as best he could, until his death in 2004.

Mam, by contrast, regarded being a housewife as her job, the home and kitchen as her territory. Her periodic bouts of ill health also precluded regular paid work, although she did take on temporary and short-term jobs that gave her some income and a degree of independence – a fact, I believe, that exacerbated the difficulties in the marital relationship. The autumn potato-picking was something that John and I shared with her. Then she took a job as a dressmaker in Grimsby, a task for which she was well trained before she married. That ended abruptly when a customer supposedly discovered a spot of blood on a wedding dress that Elsie was making, even though there was no sign whatsoever of any puncture on Mam's hands or arms.

Her lack of formal qualifications forced her into basic manual jobs. She once joined a team on a temporary contract to clean a ship in Immingham dock, but had to give that up after two days when she cut her hand pulling on a hank of steel wool. For a couple of years she worked as a home help, assigned to a family of pensioners in the village. She enjoyed getting out of our house and meeting other people, she said; and the best was that she didn't see her work immediately begin to deteriorate, as she did at home when we came in from school. And after moving to Scunthorpe, she took on teaching singing to a range of pupils, to whom she devoted a great deal of energy in return for extremely modest fees: she deliberately charged little so as to avoid having to pay income tax on her meagre earnings. This income she regarded as *her* money, and she used it to justify having a telephone in the house, against Dad's initial protests.

In retirement, they led largely separate lives, still living together, coping with each other, feeling disappointed with life, disgruntled, and, I'm sure, quite baffled – although they could not have expressed it in this way – at the social distance that had developed between themselves and their two sons. John still lived in Scunthorpe, with his wife and son; but I had moved away, following a career that brought me to places and social milieus that were beyond their knowledge and experience. I had some understanding of their life, but increasingly I too became aware of the distance that had opened up between us, particularly after I left B.G.S. in the summer of 1961.

9

Goodbye to North Lincs — Perhaps Farewell?

I left Barton Grammar school on 28 July 1961, and spent the summer waiting for my 'A' level results and working in the frozen food factory in Grimsby. It was the summer in which Billy Fury's 'Halfway to Paradise' blared from loudspeakers in the factory, and superstitious teenagers worried. Immediately after recording 'It Doesn't Matter Any More', Buddy Holly had been killed in a plane crash on 3 February 1959; in April the following year Eddie Cochran had died in a car accident in Britain after recording 'Three Steps to Heaven'. Bad things always happen in threes, don't they? Perhaps; but Billy Fury was not the third pop victim of superstition. Perhaps there was no third.

When the results came – two grade 3 (French and Latin), one grade 4 (English: my poor grasp of literature let me down), and an 'S' level in French, a result that won me a Lindsey Senior Scholarship – offers came by post from three universities to which I had applied to read Russian. Birmingham and Leeds offered places on their honours programme, while Liverpool offered a place to read General Studies including Russian, with the prospect of moving to honours Russian if I made sufficient progress with the language in the first year. After some thought, I accepted Leeds, and was overwhelmed by the range of material that subsequently arrived to prepare me for the next stage of my life.

Apart from the forms and information from the University administration concerning my registration and from the accommodation office to search for digs, all manner of student societies seemed interested in recruiting me, as did the main banks – aware, of course, that customers frequently stay with a particular bank for a lifetime. As matters turned out, Martin's Bank quickly disappeared; the National Provincial merged with the Westminster to become NatWest, which much later (and controversially) was taken over by Royal Bank of Scotland. This was all very new and exciting for someone from a family in which no one had ever handled a chequebook, but it represented a step away from my parents. Credit cards were a decade or more into the future for all but wealthy diners and Americans. My father, in his innocence, asked whether he would get a letter from the university about what I was expected to wear. He was surprised to learn that there was no required dress for a redbrick university student (this was before jeans and a sweater, perhaps accompanied by a university scarf, became the standard uniform of students across the world).

Through the accommodation office I found digs with a family in Chapel Allerton, off the Harrogate Road, and I arranged for a heavy suitcase to be sent in advance and delivered at the address by British Rail (a useful service that ended years ago). On the morning of Thursday, 28 September, my brother John accompanied me to Grimsby by bus, and he shook my hand on the platform of Grimsby Town station, on my way to a new life as a university student in Leeds. Until then, he and I had never been particularly close, but it was a somewhat emotional moment. I was leaving home. I knew I should be back in a few weeks, but I imagined I would probably not return to North Lincs to live after graduation: the demand for Russian-speakers there was likely to be modest.

That was the start of my disengagement with the region I knew as home, a process that was enhanced when a year later my parents moved to Scunthorpe from Immingham. John, too, had found a job as an office clerk in Scunthorpe, so from the summer of 1962 there were no regular opportunities to return to Immingham, where most of my primary and many secondary school friends lived. In Scunthorpe I had no friends, and acquaintances from Barton Grammar had gone away to university and dispersed, in some cases to pursue very distinguished careers across the globe. I would return to my parents' home for the university vacations, where I tried to pursue my studies in a household that understood less and less the direction my life was taking, little appreciating that reading could constitute 'work'. This increasing social distance from my family was one of the penalties of academic success, and it continued almost to a condition of estrangement from my father in later decades.

My contacts with B.G.S. became very infrequent. I returned in October

1961 for Speech Day, at which I happily received the prizes for French and Latin, and was able to thank many of my teachers for what they had done for me. And I said goodbye to Mrs Hodinott, the school secretary. In those days of carbon paper and Roneo stencils, decades before the invention of photocopying, let alone the personal computer and laser printer, year after year she had meticulously typed exam question papers for every subject and every class. For the last time in my life, I joined in singing the school song, 'Keep Faith', performed with gusto – or even *con brio* – by the whole school at the end of the proceedings. I attended one of the annual dinners of the Old Bartonians' Association, held in Scunthorpe. Very occasionally, on a visit to the family home, I would drive nostalgically over to Barton to look at the town, Baysgarth House and B.G.S. – but the school itself lost its identity in 1975 when it was amalgamated with the Beretun School at the other side of the playing fields. Out of curiosity I would follow the route of the school bus along the winding route through various villages to Immingham to visit scenes of my youth.

As the years passed I noticed changes. New highways gouged through the countryside, cutting across the roads along which I walked with my older cousins on a winter's Sunday afternoon or on which I rode my first bike, often in Dad's company, and once with Doreen, the village doctor's daughter, with whom I had a brief romantic engagement at the age of fourteen, to the extent of a bicycle ride during which I ungallantly let her inflate her own flat tyre. Such innocent pastimes would be too risky for any young person in twenty-first century North Lincolnshire.

Oil refineries have taken over fields between which I cycled to the Scout meetings in Killingholme or to try to catch fish in the river upstream from Immingham Creek. Immingham, in my day an expanding industrial village, became a real town, with civic offices and a shopping centre built on the field where we played on the swings and the roundabout and romped in the hay in the early summer. Dad's allotment was obliterated under a building site. Old terraces were torn down, including much of Battery Street, where we had enjoyed several Christmas lunches at the house of the singer Harry Adamson and his wife Annie ('Fanny' of the ferocious class discipline and the orchestral conducting technique). In becoming a town, in place of the village I had known, it established its own educational provision, so the school buses ceased to ply their separate ways to and from Barton.

Beyond Immingham, the roads were changed – straightened and

turned into dual carriageways. The railways declined in significance for the villages, and stations became more or less redundant: Brocklesby, Stallingborough, Great Coates, Grimsby Docks, New Clee. Remarkably, the line to Barton, via Ulceby, Thornton Abbey, Goxhill and New Holland, escaped Dr Beeching's axe in the 1960s and continues in service, but wicker baskets of pigeons are no longer to be seen on platforms awaiting despatch to distant parts for synchronised release. B.G.S. itself – or most of it – was eventually demolished and replaced by a small estate of upmarket housing, named Nightingale Close in memory of 'The Bird'.

The romantic symbol of the separation of the north and south banks of the Humber – the ferry service from New Holland to Hull, on which we were taken as infants to visit Santa's Grotto and sailed as teenagers to a Lonnie Donegan concert – has been retired and one of its vessels, the *Tattershall Castle*, is moored on the Thames by the Embankment, as a tourist attraction and restaurant. It was replaced by the elegance of the Humber Bridge, which was supposed to give substance to the Whitehall notion of 'Humberside' – a concept that never entered the minds, let alone the hearts, of those of us who grew up in Lindsey. An aunt of my mother's lived near Hull, but for the most part our family ties, inter-school sports contests and other links of those who lived on the Lincolnshire bank ran south to Lincoln, Caistor, Louth, Horncastle and Skegness, rather than across the water to Hull and Hessle. It was technically possible to wade across the estuary at a certain point at low tide; the Romans must have done so when Ermine Street brought them north from Lincoln to York, and I recall in the 1950s someone doing it to prove the point. There was an ancient ferry, too, indicated in the names of the villages of North and South Ferriby. But the Humber really was, and remains, the site of two distinct communities. To us Hull was a different world – but close enough to inspire most of my generation to attend universities a little further from home.

My life took a different direction. At Leeds University, I quickly discovered that my linguistic abilities were not of a standard to become a professional interpreter (a career that I had imagined for myself when I applied for admission). I developed an interest in Russian history and philosophy, and took part in political societies, notably the European Society, under whose auspices I first travelled outside the United Kingdom, to a student conference in Heidelberg.

I edited a couple of student magazines: *Stride*, the cyclostyled termly publication of the European Society, and *Sovremennik* ('The Contemporary'), produced twice a year by a Russian departmental student society named *Kruzhok* ('The Circle'). With the European Society, I was involved in organising an international student seminar in 1963, attended by students from across western Europe and addressed by, among others, Edward Heath, at the time Lord Privy Seal, and I became president of the society for the following academic year. Later, I became treasurer of the national Committee for Student European Associations.

I further developed interests in music: classical and folk, blues, jazz and contemporary. I lived on my grant, discovered wine (rather than beer) in Germany, stopped drinking tea with milk, tasted the delight of fresh (rather than tinned) pineapple, changed my hair style (to my father's disgust when he met me on my way home from the stylist), bought 'serious' Sunday newspapers, fell repeatedly and forlornly in love, and generally took up pursuits that steadily removed me from my background. With not a decent bookshop for thirty or forty miles, or high-quality theatres, galleries or concert halls, Scunthorpe and its environs had little attraction – quite apart from the lack of a need for speakers of inadequate Russian.

As my final year got under way, and my last undergraduate exams approached, I had to give some thought to my future career, and undertook preliminary actions. My father was quite upset when I explained that I didn't expect to return to North Lincs to live, since I believed there was nothing there for me. 'I'm sure if you look around you'll find some kind of job,' he said, with some irritation. And perhaps I could have – but the life would probably not have suited me. University changed me, in ways that my parents could hardly understand.

But I was quite uncertain about what I might do after graduation – assuming I succeeded in graduating. At the start of my last term, I stuck a note on the back of my door in the Henry Price Building – the first purpose-built block of student flats in the country, in which I was one of the original occupants: 'II.1 or bust'. I thought I might be capable of an upper second; a first was out of the question. Alas, my literature had always been a weakness, and without the history and philosophy I might be facing a third-class degree, if not failure. So I pursued other options. I half-heartedly looked into librarianship, at the suggestion of one of my lecturers, but it didn't really appeal, if only because my interests were not seriously 'bookish'. I applied for work in a couple of government agencies, including taking exams to become one of Her Britannic Majesty's inspectors of taxes. I imagined – or, rather, I assumed – that industry or business would not be very interested in me. In the end, I had a stroke of exceedingly good fortune.

In my final year, one of the teachers who had really inspired me at Leeds, Alfred Dressler, was taken to hospital with what proved to be terminal lung cancer. Literally from his death bed, he remarked to the lecturer who temporarily replaced him – Theodore Shanin, a Russian *émigré* who travelled fortnightly from Birmingham to give his lectures (he later became a distinguished professor and expert on the Russian peasantry) – that there were two students in the final year who, he believed, had some academic potential. One of those was myself. That was very encouraging, but I thought it would depend on an upper second, which I wasn't certain of attaining.

However, a few weeks before my final exams, in the late spring of 1965, I replied to an advertisement for a research assistant at the newly established University of Essex. It was to work on a project on the Soviet political system, and would require a reading knowledge of Russian. I was called for interview and subsequently offered the job, having ambitiously expressed my desire to pursue an academic career – something I had scarcely contemplated until that point. I gained a rather disappointing lower second and was temporarily disheartened. Such a result would now have been seen as almost akin to failure, and certainly not a springboard for any kind of postgraduate degree, let alone an academic career, so I explained apologetically to my superiors at Essex – Professor Jean Blondel and David Shapiro, who was about to transfer from Nuffield College, Oxford – that my performance had not matched my hopes. Mercifully, they were undeterred, and in October 1965 I moved to Colchester, set myself up in a bed-sit on the Maldon Road, transferred my books to the university, and started work on a project that was to prove a turning-point in my life.

As I embarked upon the research project, under the guidance of David Shapiro, reading daily copies of a Soviet newspaper and compiling a card index on individuals whose names appeared in the press, I joined the inaugural class of the MA programme in Political Behaviour. This was designed to train researchers in politics, using approaches devised since the 1950s in the United States, and enthusiastically promoted by Professor Blondel. The one-year programme consisted of lectures and seminars from October until exams in June, followed by a short dissertation over the summer. I was allowed to follow the programme over two years, to allow me to focus on the work for which the university was paying me. At the end of the taught component, I made use of my research project to base my dissertation on the Communist Party Central Committee in the republic of Moldavia (now Moldova), using some of the statistical techniques that I had learnt during the coursework.

I found this all very exciting. The Department of Government – indeed, the whole university, which had opened its doors to students in the previous year – was a vibrant place, full of intellectual energy, engaged in the discovery of new knowledge through research. The library had a very impressive collection of books, journals and newspapers from the Soviet Union, and had a policy of very open access. I was a member of a group of well-educated young people who were better trained than I was in the social sciences, and I found their company exhilarating. It was a long way from the studies of literature that had dogged my academic performance throughout grammar school and my undergraduate years. I was not a brilliant student, but at least a competent one, and I managed to produce a dissertation that in part was subsequently published in the leading scholarly journal for Soviet studies.

After two years, I went to Moldavia on a British Council scholarship, set up as part of the Anglo-Soviet Cultural Exchange Agreement that had been running for a number of years. For the first time, the Soviet authorities, in the early Brezhnev years, allowed British postgraduates to spend a year outside the main centres of Moscow and Leningrad: one language student went to Voronezh; an economist was sent to Tashkent, in Uzbekistan; and to my surprise I was assigned to Kishinev, since the focus of my research was the republic of Moldavia. In a stay of nine enjoyable but arduous months, during which I was formally attached to the Institute of Economics of the Academy of Sciences, but living in a very basic student hostel alongside university students of foreign languages, I gathered sufficient materials to turn into a doctoral dissertation on my return. I also improved my knowledge of Russian far beyond the standard I had attained in Leeds, and picked up a fair amount of Romanian (although written in the Cyrillic script and officially called 'Moldavian').

I learned to live on my own – I was the only westerner in the city for most of the time – and to deal with a suspicious if not hostile bureaucracy. I spent a month in the city of Tiraspol, which decades later became the capital of the self-styled Dniester Moldovan Republic (also known as Transnistria), paid visits to British friends in Moscow at Christmas and Easter, took a train to Odessa a couple of times, was shown something of the Moldavian countryside – during one trip, we inadvertently came across a prison, complete with nearby quarry – and at the end of the year spent a relaxing week in Yalta, the pearl of the Black Sea, before heading home on a Danubian river cruise as far as Vienna, through Romania, Bulgaria, Hungary and Czechoslovakia, and thence homeward by train, spending a few days in Vienna, Munich and Cologne on the way.

MOLDAVIA, JUNE 1968

This all convinced me that I had personal experiences that could inform a teacher of Soviet politics, helping to bring alive lectures on political institutions and structures. So during a year back at Essex, which I devoted to preparing my notes for processing by computer in a numerical analysis of the political elite of Tiraspol, I applied for academic positions. After several unsuccessful interviews, I was eventually offered a post of Junior Lecturer in Trinity College, Dublin, which I accepted.

On 30 September 1969, I arrived on the boat from Holyhead to begin a new life that seemed a long way from North Lincs, Barnetby, Immingham, Barton, Grimsby, Leeds, Colchester and the other places where I had grown up and spent my formative years. I told everyone, myself included, that I was going to Dublin for three to five years. But I have stayed. I was apparently successful as a lecturer. I managed to pursue my research and to publish academic articles and books that attracted attention. Some of my work was published in Japan, in Indonesia, in South Korea, in Germany, Italy, Finland and Belarus, in addition to more usual publication for English-speaking scholars in Britain and the United States. I was elected a Fellow of Trinity College in 1978, followed by promotion to the rank of Associate Professor, and in 1981 went to Lafayette College, Easton, Pennsylvania, as a visiting professor for a year, at the end of which I drove across the United States and back. I also paid further visits to the Soviet Union, including a couple of months in Moscow in 1975, and visits as a tourist to Leningrad, Moscow, L'vov, Kishinev, Odessa, Kiev and elsewhere. In the summer of 1976 I went to Warsaw for the first time, to spend a month learning the rudiments of the Polish language, and acquiring an affection for the Polish people and their country that I have never felt for the Russians, despite my respect for their cultural achievements.

In 1989 I enjoyed the great experience of a fellowship at the Netherlands Institute of Advanced Studies (NIAS), where I was part of a team examining the unfolding collapse of the communist system in Eastern Europe. For an academic this was the closest one came to heaven without actually dying. On a spring morning, the day began with a pleasant cycle ride through tulip fields in full bloom, followed by research work in one's own office, a communal lunch to socialise with twenty or so other scholars of various disciplines, perhaps a cycle ride through the dunes for a stroll on the beach, then further work until 5 o'clock when some of the group might break off for a glass of wine and a game of croquet. Then further study for a couple of hours before cycling home for supper. The NIAS building was open all hours, so if one wanted to work late (as I often did), that posed no problem. I visited some of Holland's pretty little towns – Gouda, Delft, Leiden, Groningen, Utrecht – and enjoyed the art galleries and the streetscapes of Amsterdam and The Hague. I was sad to take the boat from Rotterdam to Hull on my way home – but it gave me a chance to revisit my family in Scunthorpe.

Thereafter, I was promoted to a personal chair, as Professor of Soviet Government – a title that I had to ask the College authorities to change within a year or two, as the Soviet Union collapsed and became history. I was not, after all, a historian, and interviewers on Irish radio asking about events in the former communist world started joking about whether I still had a job now that there was no longer a Soviet Union.

I undertook editorial work, continuing from where I had left off with my undergraduate magazines. I used the knowledge of grammar, punctuation and style learned from Henry Treece to act as style editor of a new journal, *The Journal of Communist Studies*, founded by a group of friends and professional colleagues in Britain. For twenty-seven years, I read every word of this quarterly journal, correcting the spelling, amending the punctuation, finding more accurate or elegant ways of saying things in English, and turning the writing of non-native speakers of our language into standard British prose. It was a challenge, and sometimes tedious, but it was something that I seemed able to do competently, and I gained a great sense of satisfaction from helping young or foreign scholars get into print. I even developed the skills that began with the John Bull Printing Set, and used a computer to type-set three dozen or more books. Writing, editing, typesetting and indexing became an important part of my professional life, and as a hobby I even dabbled in book binding. One never knows when skills or knowledge will be useful.

My international contacts continued. For a decade or so, I was involved in dealing with visiting students from around the world, and in sending Irish students for a year at various Continental universities. At the turn of the century, I was involved in a project with French colleagues at a private university in Minsk, capital of Belarus, which ran for three years. And through my career in Trinity College I met the world-renowned Russian musicians Shostakovich and Rostropovich, Irish presidents De Valera, Robinson and McAleese, the former Soviet leader Mikhail Gorbachev, many visiting prime ministers and ministers who visited Trinity College or the Institute of International and European Affairs in Dublin, and on one memorable occasion in March 1985 – memorable to me, at least, but hardly to her, given the subsequent trajectory of her distinguished career – a *tête-à-tête* dinner in a Thai restaurant in London with Condoleezza Rice, years before she became US Secretary of State. I have certainly enjoyed experiences that would never have come my way without the education that began in North Lincs – or, indeed, if I had stayed in North Lincs.

As part of all this, I confess, I even changed my mode of speech. I found when I first came across individuals whose native language was not English – at Leeds University, and later in the Soviet Union and elsewhere

– that they found a regional British accent difficult to understand. Not only vocabulary, but the 'flat' Northern way of speaking in general, with the short *a* in 'grass' and 'after' and other peculiarities of our pronunciation. Since I had studied phonetics, starting in B.G.S., I knew what I needed to do to make myself more universally understood, so I did it. Along the way, I also encountered a way of discovering whether an individual comes from north or south of a line that links the Bristol Channel with The Wash: ask them to count – 1, 2, 3 – and pay attention to the first: do they say 'wonn' (North) or 'wunn' (South)? But since I know the trick, I can disguise my origins if I wish. So, returning to my home turf, I know I no longer speak as a native – but other native speakers of Humberside English also know I'm not one of them. My speech today is somewhat nondescript, difficult to place, not sure of where it or I belong.

I also dropped certain expressions, for the same reason. For example, most English people outside a certain area of the north don't understand the word 'mardy', used of a fractious or irritable child. They are also surprised at the notion that one can starve with cold as well as hunger – because they forgot, centuries ago, that to starve meant to die; if they knew this, they might find the expression as useful as we do in Lincolnshire. Or did. Half a century after I left the county, I'm not sure how much the local dialect has changed. The kind of phrases that I heard from the lips of the old-timer on Beacock's farm in 1961 were already on the way out. So I wonder whether the younger generation in south Yorkshire still uses 'thou' – as in ' 'Ast a bin to t' market?' ('Hast thou been to the market?') that I heard in Mexborough on an occasion when my mother was competing there in the music festival. In the past three decades, Australian soap operas on television have impinged across Britain and the world on the cadences of young people's speech, to the extent that many statements now sound like questions. I now wonder how much of what I grew up thinking of as 'normal' has already been displaced.

The fact is that, throughout these years living as an expatriate, my contacts with my youth dwindled. Despite being plugged into the motorway network, and connected with Hull by a bridge, reaching North Lincs is still not easy. The position of the Humber means that main transport routes from north to south were laid out to the west of the county, and there are no major cities that have an airport for easy access. Thanks to motorways and the Humber bridge, Yorkshire is now more accessible from the south bank, and from the west; but reaching

Scunthorpe, Immingham, Grimsby or Barton from Ireland remains a major trek, and without a car it is difficult to get around.

I stayed in touch by Christmas card and letter with Chad, my former Latin master, and his wife Edith, who had struggled (with some embarrassment, as she has recently confessed) to teach me literature. But, while I frequently visited other parts of the United Kingdom, and continue to do so, my main contact with North Lincs has been through my immediate family, who lived in Scunthorpe, and I steadily visited them a couple of times a year. My trips eastwards from Scunthorpe, in the direction of the Wolds and my early life, including aunts and uncles and cousins in Grimsby and Cleethorpes, became very infrequent, so I didn't witness the massive developments taking place that have rendered the old centres of Grimsby and Immingham quite unrecognisable.

My Grandmother's house, at 30 Clayton Street, Grimsby, was demolished years ago, making way for the Riverhead Centre, now the Freshney Place Centre, where memory of the street is retained in the vestigial 'Clayton Walk'. All the details remain in my head: the terrace of Clayton Street itself, the alleyway between the houses, the tiny garden to the rear, where we normally entered the house, the parlour with my Auntie Jean's collection of ceramic Toby jugs, the add-on bathroom with its gas geyser at the very back of the house through the kitchen and jutting out into the garden (was it a converted coal-shed?), the front room that we rarely entered, and the walk to the railway station and the bus station behind. Through Brewery Street or Silver Street, past Gough & Davy, where my mother used to order sheet music and I bought her a present of Kathleen Ferrier singing Handel's 'Spring is Coming' on a 78 r.p.m. shellac record; sometimes I would make a detour, passing along Flottergate and through the Old Market Place, avoiding Victoria Street with its department stores Guy & Smith and Lawson & Stockdale. Further along Victoria Street there was the Monkey, Pig and Pie Shop, and on Freeman Street Holder Brothers, for music and electrical goods; a shoe shop on Pasture Street, just beyond the level crossing, where for several years the males in the family were shod; Steel's fish and chips on Freeman Street market – my mother's favourite spot for lunch during shopping excursions to Grimsby (where I learned the practice of leaving a sixpenny piece on the table as a tip). In the middle of Freeman Street a branch of Woolworth's, which still sold a single screw or a couple of nails, all displayed on counters with compartments from which the customer picked what was required.

On Alexandra Road there was Dan Bunn, the barber, where we went for our fortnightly trim before Dad discovered Sid Heyhoe on Daubney Street, Cleethorpes, close to my grandfather's house on Barcroft Street. Near to Granddad's was Sidney Park, where my brother and I used to wander round the pond – once in the company of a younger cousin who walked into the water while pulling a twig attached to a string: I was blamed by my Uncle Herbert, my mother's brother who lived nearby, for this mishap. Two adoptive 'aunts', my mother's childhood friends and acquaintances, lived in Cleethorpes: 'Auntie' Eve on Harrington Street, behind Blundell Park, the Grimsby Town football ground – from her house it was possible to follow the success of the Mariners with the roar and groans of the crowd; and 'Auntie' Muriel, on Oxford Street, near enough to the promenade to take in paying guests from Sheffield or Leicester or Manchester in the summer. Apparently my grandfather had proposed marriage to her following his wife's death; she had declined, and did not regret it – although Elsie and her brothers and sisters did.

In my mind I still smell the hops and barley from Hewitt's brewery, and the sickly odour of Tickler's jam factory, which reminds me in turn of our primary school headmaster, Mr Meakin. In my boyhood, the buses used to stop at Park Street, the boundary between Grimsby and Cleethorpes. Each town had its own transport system, until a united company was agreed and it became possible to travel from one town the other on a single bus – including the trolley buses, powered by overhead lines, a mode of transport that I encountered in the Soviet Union and Romania years after they had ceased to ply the roads of Grimsby. And the clogs with their heavily studded wooden soles in the windows of the docks area – worn by 'lumpers' who heaved the boxes of wet fish around the fish market.

Much of this, still clearly fixed in my mind's eye, passed into history decades ago. The fish docks that defined the town are sadly deserted, most of the trawlers now gone, and the streets that I walked on Saturdays have been replaced by massive warehouses in a town that calls itself the frozen-food capital of Europe.

Up-river, at Immingham, my former home on Princess Street still exists, six decades and more since we first occupied it, and some of the neighbouring streets retain their familiarity. I walk along them today, and remember friends who lived there: Dave Hall over there, a family that had its own transport – a motorbike and sidecar; Dave followed me to Leeds University, where he read economics; the Raithbys, a couple of doors from them; up the street the house where Raymond Bennett lived – the only boy I remember having a schoolboy fight with; he too later went to Leeds University. Gone, though, in these days of mobile phones, is the street's single telephone kiosk, from which I occasionally reported that the school bus had not turned up, and 38 or so pupils would not be arriving at school that day. On Pelham Road stands the house of the vicar, where 'Philbert' Sowerby and the rest of us in the Black Diamonds practised for hours (and occasionally frolicked with his female cousins from Gainsborough). And the homes of classmates and girlfriends and other girls I think I fancied – all still there.

But many of my old haunts have disappeared under new streets and houses and offices as the town has expanded and matured. The collection of prefabricated bungalows at the bottom of Princess Street – an emergency solution to the post-war housing shortage – has long gone; most of the site is now a car park. With their demolition no doubt went the memory of Miss Tweddle, the village midwife, who did her rounds on her district nurse bicycle, carrying her little black leather case to minister to the needs of expectant mothers, including the occasional unfortunate schoolgirl who had 'got into trouble', as the saying had it. Nurse Tweddle knew practically every child in the village, since she had delivered most of them.

Also long gone: 'Jesus' Jackson, an unkempt, somewhat eccentric son of the soil who lived on a farm near the church, a figure of fun to us children who gave him the nickname because of his flowing beard; 'Three-wheeler Jack', who rode a tricycle because of a limp; and Henry, the epileptic who had never really grown up, a kindly village idiot known to everyone, including all the children.

They belong to a world that has passed, even as some features have scarcely altered. Saint Andrew's church, to which the village has now encroached, contains the sadly neglected triple grave of Herbert Meakin, his wife and her sister, Miss Summers, individuals who had a profound influence on the lives of hundreds of children, myself included, now forgotten by today's inhabitants of what is no longer a village. At least the memory of Mr Meakin, headmaster, councillor, founding member of the Immingham cricket club, and for many years a distinguished member of the community, is preserved in the name of what strikes me as a rather charmless block of retirement and sheltered flats on the edge of town beyond Pilgrim Avenue and the end of Margaret Street.

Barnetby, too, remains in some of its essence unchanged. Our little cottage on the King's Road is still inhabited, but the privy across the yard has been replaced by proper plumbing, and the gardens that were once an essential part of all four households' provisioning are now unused. The malt kiln that dominated the view from the garden fell into severe disrepair and has been demolished. Cockerel Havercroft's house still stands, but his orchard has been built upon. Silver Street, Victoria Road – much appears the same; even Kirkby's shop, on the corner, remains a grocery store, now turned supermarket. But at the other end of the village, past the church and my first school, much building has taken place. The school itself is now a block of flats (elegant ones, I like to think), its front entrance reconstructed beyond recognition, and the alley that led us to Victoria Road following 'Mr Wolf' (Miss Freeston) has been truncated by a small housing development.

Barton – well, I hardly knew Barton, despite attending B.G.S. for seven years. It is a very pretty town, and attractive for outsiders to settle in, with easy access today to the facilities of Hull, across the bridge. Those who grew up there will be more aware of the changes than I am. Certainly, the rope factory no longer functions, but has been converted into a flourishing arts centre, The Ropewalk; Elswick-Hopper cycles struggled for years before eventually closing (but my trusty Elswick-Hopper bike, bought in Dublin in the 1970s, is still just about road-worthy). Baysgarth House is now host to a museum that houses quite a few familiar objects from B.G.S.: the oak chair with the school coat-of-arms carved and set into its back that was used by the Chairman of the Governors, Dr Kirk, on speech days, and the two honours boards, made by Mr Millet, the woodwork master, with crests painted by Henry Treece. But the school itself no longer exists – except for the new block that was just beginning to rise on the 'cabbage patch' at the time I made my vote of thanks as Head Boy on Speech Day 1960.

With awe I look at the honours boards, now in the museum. My own name may appear as a recipient of a Lindsey Senior Scholarship in 1961, a good year: one State Scholarship, five Lindsey Seniors, and a National Coal Board Scholarship, all shared among five individuals, including the star, Stuart Aaron, who had joined the school somewhat later. But then I consider the illustrious names of pupils from previous years. Colin

Smart, Head Boy in the year I arrived in the school. He had already attained a Lindsey Senior in 1954 and in the following year won a State Scholarship. I was pleasantly surprised, as a final-year undergraduate in Leeds University in 1965, to see a photo of him on the cover of the *Sunday Times* magazine. After leaving B.G.S., he had taken a degree in chemistry and become a researcher for the industrial giant I.C.I. Equally brilliant, and with a very similar academic profile, was Jane Stockdale, Head Girl in that same year. Looking back even further, the name of Marjorie Boulton stands out. The daughter of the first headmaster, in 1941 she had won a State Scholarship, a Lindsey Senior Scholarship, an Exhibition to Somerville College, Oxford, and a Lowman Memorial Prize; she had obtained a doctorate from Oxford and become a poet and prolific author in English and Esperanto. Enid Brice, daughter of 'Billo', had won a State Scholarship, a Lindsey Senior Scholarship and a Scholarship to Royal Holloway College, University of London (and she compiled a history of B.G.S., published in 2002).

Those distinguished scholars were some years ahead of me, but there were others whose faces I have carried in my mind for over half a century who have gone on to considerable achievement in many fields. A glance at the photos in old copies of *The Bartonian* reminds me of them. John Brice, Enid's younger brother, Head Boy in 1956, cricket captain, and winner of a Lindsey Senior followed by a State Scholarship. John ('Junk') Kirk, Head Boy a year later, football and cricket captain, awarded a Lindsey Senior Scholarship in 1958. Also a couple of years ahead of me was the writer Ted Lewis, whose novel *Jack's Return Home* was turned into the crime thriller film *Get Carter*, starring Michael Caine.

From my own year, Bill West (then known by his other name, Roger), read science in London and spent part of his career as a safety inspector of nuclear power stations in the Soviet Union: we may conceivably have been in the country at the same time – who knows? He can still quote Virgil in Latin. Brian Moss was one of the more interesting – some might even say 'eccentric' – of my near-contemporaries: in school he was a keen photographer, he monitored the rain gauge and the maximum-and-minimum thermometer inside the school's weather station, fitted a radio to his bike, and led a group of boys in search of a 'priest hole' – a secret chamber to hide persecuted Catholic priests in Elizabethan England – inside Baysgarth House; after leaving B.G.S. he trained as a teacher, lived in Zambia, cycled across the United States, and has long served as a local councillor in Warwickshire. Michael Baldwin, another scientist from a year ahead of me (I remember he received the scores of Beethoven's 32 piano sonatas as a school prize), trained in chemistry at Sheffield University, moved to Canada and later the United States, and subsequently was appointed vice-president of technology in a major American chemical corporation. From the same year, Roger Ebbatson read English at Sheffield, and became a professor, a prolific author and renowned expert on Tennyson, Hardy and Lawrence. Other distinguished Bartonians followed in the footsteps of the generation of the 1950s, including the Labour Member of Parliament for Ipswich in the 1990s, Jamie Cann.

There were probably scores of others who had an impact on the wider world – in Canada, Australia, Portugal, France or elsewhere – and lots more who made a contribution closer to home. Many former pupils that I know of became teachers in North Lincs, thereby giving rather more back to their home county than I have done. Others joined the armed forces, became doctors or hairdressers, police officers or nurses (despite Norman Goddard's dismissive attitude: to him nursing was not a 'profession'), ran the family farm, or found some other line of business or work that allowed them to use their education. Just hearing about these Old Bartonians evokes in me a sense of great satisfaction. It is quite amazing that a small grammar school, in what many in the rest of Britain would see as a backwater – the Humber's south bank – could have engaged such inspiring teachers and produced such a range of successful pupils. It was without doubt a fine school.

Visits to my boyhood region provide a whiff of nostalgia – but my life has taken me in different, unexpected directions. Without B.G.S., it would not have been possible. Billo, Chad, Henry Treece, Norman Goddard, Miss Pollard, Freddie Manning, 'Horace' Hopley – these and other devoted teachers who came and went during my seven years in the school set me on my way, taking over from Miss Freeston, Miss Beverly and 'Nobby' Clark in St. Barnabas' Primary, then 'Fanny' Adamson, Miss Summers and Herbert Meakin in Immingham Church of England school. They all helped shape me, and I look back with affection and gratitude to them all.

And also to my parents. They comprehended little of the effect of education in forming – in fact, *transforming* – a human being. Education gave me opportunities to explore ideas and gain experiences in a world of which they knew practically nothing. So I grew away from them as I grew away from North Lincs, and they were, I think, puzzled by the growing differences between themselves and the person they still thought of as their 'little boy'. Communication became less easy as the years passed. This led to strains within the family, and sometimes the irritation made itself felt. Their life was a hard one, even harsh. They always did their best, without realising what they were contributing to. And, to their eternal credit, they allowed me to dream, and to gain the confidence and the ability that they lacked, to seize the opportunities and pursue their own dreams.

It was not accidental that, after leaving B.G.S., I pursued a career that entailed languages and the study of foreign politics and cultures, and I have been very contented to make lifelong friends around the world. A proud moment was when I was able to invite a friend from Moscow, a professor at Moscow State University, to stay with me when the Soviet Union started opening up in the late 1980s, and some years later another close friend from what had become the independent Republic of Moldova.

By then I had become a fixture in Ireland, where I was honoured in 1999 to receive a medal from the Russian embassy marking the bicentenary of the birth of Russia's great poet, Alexander Pushkin, for my contribution to Irish–Russian cultural relations. I was even more honoured in 2011 to receive a similar medal from the Polish Foundation for Tolerance, awarded to distinguished Poles and foreigners 'for the promotion of tolerance'. I abhor narrow nationalism, and I suppose if pressed I would reject the principle that statehood is the only valid form of self-expression for an ethnic group. I have seen – and still do witness – the hatred engendered by this idea. Even in B.G.S., I was ashamed at the notion, once expressed in a school debate, that we should prevent West Indians from entering the United Kingdom 'for their own sake'. Ignoring the question of justice to the descendants of victims of the British slave trade, the idea that the British people were so xenophobic that foreigners should be protected by exclusion was an extremely uncomfortable thought. The notion still offends me.

Many years later, I was shocked, as a European, to hear the president of the American Political Science Association declare, at a conference in Italy, that for most Americans the natural condition of Europe is war. Yet when I thought about it, I saw that he was right – and the warring continues. Not on the scale of the two world wars that began in Europe, but

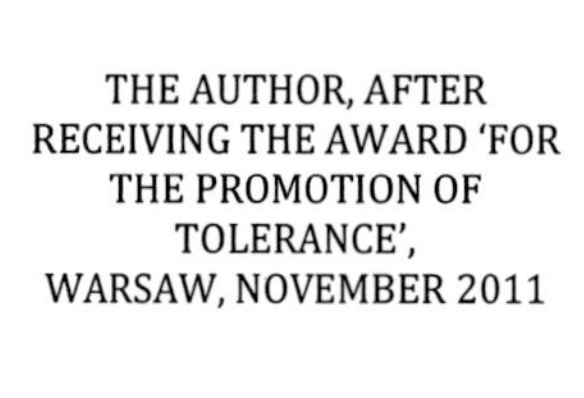

THE AUTHOR, AFTER RECEIVING THE AWARD 'FOR THE PROMOTION OF TOLERANCE', WARSAW, NOVEMBER 2011

certainly still within Europe, and even more so in countries that were created by Europe on other continents.

To this extent – and it is a considerable extent – my continued education and my life's experience have led me to reject many of the values that were implicit in the education I received in my primary schools: the glory of Empire, pride in seeing all the pink on the map, textbook illustrations of colonials in pith helmets with their foot on the head of a lion they had shot, or even the servile relationship on the Camp coffee bottle label (subtly altered in recent years so that the Indian servant appears a little less obsequious towards his British officer). I have grown away from those values through life-long education.

By the time I entered B.G.S., that was already beginning to fade, with the independence of former colonies already under way (and it continued when the Gold Coast, the homeland of my penfriend 'Yankee Boy', became Ghana in 1957). Even in Immingham C of E School, Mr Meakin, who had proudly served in the army in India, taught us that the new queen was not 'Empress of India', whereas her father, George VI, had been designated emperor.

Having lived in Ireland for two-thirds of my life, I appreciate better than I did before what it feels like to be on the receiving end of British policy – just as I have discovered similar sentiments towards Russia when

I have been in Moldova, Poland or Ukraine. Relations between big powers and their smaller neighbours, whether or not they have acquired statehood, are a problem that both fascinates and perplexes me.

I was proud in two senses when the Queen paid a highly successful visit to Ireland in May 2011. I was proud, first of all, that Her Majesty performed so professionally – bowing her head longer than was strictly necessary at the memorial to the Irish who had died asserting Irish independence from Britain; beginning her address at the state banquet with a salutation in the Irish language; and obviously enjoying meetings with Irish people. But I was equally proud that a nation among whom I had lived for so many years rose to the occasion in a manner that many in Ireland thought it was incapable of doing – the crisp drill of the army colours party before the head of a state that does pageantry so magnificently; the legendary informality of the Irish that quickly put the royal party at their ease; and the showcasing of scientific, sporting and musical endeavour that has raised the Irish nation from servility under frankly oppressive British rule over many generations to an equal partner standing alongside the United Kingdom in the European Union and other international forums.

I have been part of this transformation, may even have contributed to it, and I derive a measure of satisfaction from this. The Irish have, after all, made an enormous contribution to the development of my own country and county over the past three centuries, and continue to do so.

All of this has brought me a long way from my modest origins in North Lincs. Barton Grammar School changed me, and my subsequent education and life experiences have continued to turn me into whatever I am today. Quite apart from physical changes, I am not the person who grew up near the south bank of the Humber. And I return now to a world that is very different from the one that shaped me and remains in detail in my mind.

In my boyhood years, I never imagined becoming a professor: indeed, I'm not sure when I became aware that professors existed. B.G.S. hardly encouraged me to think of myself as an academic high-flyer: bright enough, so I could reasonably aim to teach French in a grammar school. But I am not certain that I should have been successful at that. I always lacked the patience, the imagination, the empathy, to command the respect and affection of teenagers. I sensed this long before I had to make career-defining choices. I was particularly deficient in the literary skills required to become an effective teacher of modern languages in a comprehensive school, and I still possess some of my sixth-form exercise books that prove the point. I was not alone in regretting the custom of encouraging pupils to select their 'best' school subjects for university study. In choosing Russian, I rebelled to some extent, but no one encouraged politics, economics or law, to the regret of some of my friends.

Yet continuity remains. I have always stuck to a principle that my father passed on, each time we shook hands on my departure from visiting home (that was the extent of our intimacy): 'Do your best'. That is the most anyone can do – but it is also the least anyone *should* do. I wonder, too, whether I was imbued with a sense of obligation, loyalty or duty that was embodied in the school motto and song: 'Keep Faith', an English version of the Latin *Semper fidelis*. I have always tried not to let people down. I have not always succeeded, and this has led to embarrassment and disappointment. But in striving to achieve things, I have been fairly successful. I have also, through my work, lived in interesting places, done some interesting things, met some interesting people – genuine movers and shakers – without, however, becoming one of that impressive company. With a few exceptions, I have not made things happen. So my 'legacy' includes no Irish Institute of Russian and East European Studies, which someone with more drive, or more contacts, or more vision than I possess might have established and nurtured. Reticence as an outsider in Ireland is part of the explanation, but I fear other genetic traits have held me back – and there's not much I could have done about that.

I do feel proud to be part of such a distinguished company of former B.G.S. pupils, to have made a career in the wider world, to have won friends in various countries, to have enjoyed professional collaboration with international scholars, to have contributed to teaching the rising generation in Britain, Ireland, the United States and even Belarus, to have helped others reach their potential. In short, I am gratified to have made a difference – as I sincerely hope and believe I have – to people's lives, just as my family, my teachers, Scoutmasters, work colleagues and classmates contributed to my own development. They helped me to find my own level, and my education has continued throughout my life. Unable to return and feel truly 'at home' in North Lincs – or even in England, come to that – I look back in gratitude and affection to the place that gave me a start in life.